*Instructor's Manual and Test Bank*
*to accompany*

# CRIMINAL LAW AND PROCEDURE
## Fourth Edition

## Daniel E. Hall, J.D., Ed.D.

THOMSON
DELMAR LEARNING

Australia Canada Mexico Singapore Spain United Kingdom United States

## WEST LEGAL STUDIES

Instructor's Manual and Test Bank to accompany
Criminal Law and Procedure, 4E
Daniel E. Hall, J.D., Ed.D

COPYRIGHT © 2004 by Delmar Learning.
West Legal Studies is an imprint of Delmar, a division of
Thomson Learning, Inc. Thomson Learning™ is a trademark
used herein under license.

Printed in the United States
  2  3  4  5  XXX  07 06 05 04

For more information contact Delmar Learning
5 Maxwell Drive, Clifton Park, NY 12065-2919.

Or find us on the World Wide Web at
http://www.westlegalstudies.com

For permission to use material from this text or product, contact
us by:
Tel   (800) 730-2214
Fax   (800) 730-2215
www.thomsonrights.com

Library of Congress Card Catalog Number —200346287

ISBN 1-4018-1560-X

### NOTICE TO THE READER

Publisher does not warrant or guarantee any of the products described herein or perform any independent analysis in connection with any of the product information contained herein. Publisher does not assume, and expressly disclaims, any obligation to obtain and include information other than that provided to it by the manufacturer.

The reader is notified that this text is an educational tool, not a practice book. Since the law is in constant change, no rule or statement of law in this book should be relied upon for any service to any client. The reader should always refer to standard legal sources for the current rule or law. If legal advice or other expert assistance is required, the services of the appropriate professional should be sought.

The Publisher makes no representation or warranties of any kind, including but not limited to, the warranties of fitness for particular purpose or merchantability, nor are any such representations implied with respect to the material set forth herein, and the publisher takes no responsibility with respect to such material. The publisher shall not be liable for any special, consequential, or exemplary damages resulting, in whole or part, from the readers' use of, or reliance upon, this material.

# CONTENTS

## PART I   ANSWERS TO CHAPTER REVIEW QUESTIONS AND PROBLEMS

## PART II   TEST BANK

# INTRODUCTION

This guide is designed to assist the instructor in the use of *Criminal Law and Procedure,* Fourth Edition, by Daniel E. Hall. Included herein are: an outline of chapters; the answers to the questions and problems that appear at the end of every chapter in the text; a test bank organized by chapter; and an answer key to the test bank. For organizational convenience, those cases that appear in the text (in excerpt form) are noted in the chapter outline by abbreviated case name.

The questions in the test bank are exclusively objective: multiple choice or true/false. Those instructors interested in discussion or essay-type questions are referred to the problems that appear at the end of every chapter.

All questions that appear in the text and test bank have been written by me. Having used instructor's guides that have poorly drafted questions, as well as questions from material not covered in the text, I have made a conscious effort to draft clear, straightforward questions that cover the basic principles discussed in the text.

Daniel E. Hall

# OUTLINE OF CHAPTERS

# PART II CRIMINAL PROCEDURE

## CHAPTER 1

### REVIEW QUESTIONS

1. The executive branch is responsible for enforcing the laws of the land. This involves the detection and investigation of alleged criminal law violations and the prosecution of those believed to have violated criminal prohibitions.

2. A court of record is one that employs some means of keeping a verbatim transcript of its proceedings. It is common to use stenotype or audio recording.

3. Three definitions of jurisdiction appear in the text:

   1. The authority of a governmental unit over a policy area, person, or thing.

   2. Authority of a court to hear a case.

   3. The geographical location where a governmental unit resides.

   A court of general jurisdiction has authority to hear a variety of cases, both civil and criminal. Most state trial courts have general jurisdiction. Courts with limited jurisdiction may only hear cases within a specific subject matter.

4. Civil law seeks to compensate those injured by another. Criminal law seeks to punish those who violate criminal law. Criminal law uses punishment as a remedy, and civil law uses damages or other financial compensation. (Both, on occasion, use injunctive relief.)

5. Anyone may file a civil suit. However, this is not true of criminal actions, where initiation must be by a public official. This is because injury to another civilly is viewed as a private wrong, while injuring another in violation of criminal law is viewed as a public wrong. Of course, many actions can lead to both civil and criminal actions.

6. Compensatory damages are the amount of money required to compensate a victim for his or her actual loss. Punitive damages are the amount exceeding actual damages. Although punitives appear criminal, they are often permitted in civil litigation.

7. This question is one that requires the students to render their personal positions. However, the issue that should be addressed is that punitives appear to have a criminal element in that they seek to punish, not compensate. You may want to discuss the possible due process question, to wit: If punitives are criminal in nature, why are defendants not permitted established criminal law protections (i.e., proof beyond a reasonable doubt)?

8. Blameworthy; guilt.

### REVIEW PROBLEMS

1. This question is intended to test students' understanding of federalism, and, more specifically, how the Supremacy Clause operates in the United States' federalist form of government. Obviously, the state statute fails. *Roe v. Wade* is a decision that is premised upon the Fourteenth Amendment of the United States Constitution, and, as such, states may not encroach upon this protected civil liberty.

2. This question is different from number one in that students must choose between state constitutional law and federal constitutional law. For the reasons above the state constitutional provision is invalid.

3. This question is intended to test students' understanding of federalism, and, more specifically, the Tenth Amendment. If the regulation of county roads is one exclusively within state jurisdiction, then the United States Congress may not declare that it possesses jurisdiction over that subject. Accordingly, the defense would be lack of jurisdiction by the federal government.

1

# CHAPTER 2

## REVIEW QUESTIONS

1. Civil liberties are individual, personal rights. The United States Constitution protects many such rights, and the student is required to list any two. The freedoms of speech and religion were specifically mentioned in the text.

2. Common law is a body of unwritten law (in the sense that statutory law is written), which develops from the custom and practices of a community, as recognized by judicial decisions. Stare decisis ("Let the decision stand") is a legal doctrine giving respect to judicial decisions by having later cases follow the law as set in earlier cases. The earlier case looked to for a legal conclusion is known as precedent. The common law would be no more than a set of inconsistent opinions if it were not for stare decisis.

3. Every state has its own judicial system that is free to interpret state law matters differently.

4. "There is no crime if there is no law (statute)." It is important in criminal law because the doctrine can work to prohibit the creation of crimes by courts, which was common under the common law. Generally, the doctrine requires the existence of a statute to impose criminal liability. Additionally, the statute must be enacted prior to the time that the criminal act occurred. This principle is enforced through the due process clauses of the Fifth and Fourteenth Amendments to the Constitution of the United States (many states have comparable provisions in their constitutions).

5. The principle of legality is a phrase that describes what is discussed in the answer to question number four. It is a due process concept requiring that criminal prohibitions be written, that it exist prior to when the alleged act took place, and that such laws be precise. The common law, when used in the creation of crimes, violates this principle because the declaration that the act is criminal does not occur until after the act has been taken. This appears to violate the due process clauses of the Fifth and Fourteenth amendments, as no notice that the act could be punished was provided.

6. Even in such jurisdictions, the common law is useful. First, in many cases legislatures simply adopt the common-law definition when codifying the crime. In those instances, the opinions of courts are very helpful in understanding the crime, as it is assumed that the legislature did not intend to alter the common law.

Second, if a legislature does not set a penalty for violation of a criminal prohibition, then the common-law penalty may be applied.

Third, many procedures established under the common law continue to be valid.

7. Most criminal law is created by legislatures. The written laws of the United States Congress and the many state legislatures are known as statutes or codes. Note that administrative bodies are increasingly responsible for the creation of criminal prohibitions.

8. Ordinances are the written law of local governmental bodies, such as city and county councils.

9. The written laws of administrative agencies are called regulations, or administrative rules.

10. Courts establish rules controlling the processing of cases. These rules govern procedural aspects of the law, not substantive. Generally, the rules supplement the rules of procedure established by the legislature. Court rules, for the most part, may not conflict with legislative mandates.

11. The Constitution of the United States is the highest form of the law in the land. As such, it should appear at the apex. A division should then be drawn between those powers belonging to the states and those falling under federal jurisdiction. The result is a hierarchy wherein the United States Code and federal administrative regulations follow the Constitution in the federal system. As to states, the order should be: The Constitution of the United States, state constitutions, state statutes, state administrative regulations, and ordinances.

## REVIEW PROBLEMS

1. The paradox is true because in a state of anarchy (the absence of government) there would be great instability and insecurity. Without government, people would be free to injure one another without fear of recourse, except for private retribution.

In short, people would live in constant fear of one another. Government, and government control, have the effect of stabilizing a society. It is all of society gathering its combined force to prevent behavior deemed dangerous or improper. Each individual member of a society gives up a certain measure of freedom to behave as he or she may wish, but such freedom is given up in exchange for a safer, more predictable, and stable society. Obviously, each society is different in what civil rights are relinquished by the people to their government (which represents an increase in governmental power) and what rights are retained by the people.

2. The purposes for punishing criminals are:

A. Specific deterrence—those who are convicted and punished are specifically deterred from future misconduct.

B. General deterrence—all members of society are deterred from misconduct when individuals are punished for wrongdoing.

C. Incapacitation—criminal conduct is prevented (against society as a whole) by making it impossible for those convicted to commit future crimes. This is most often accomplished by incarceration, although death is another form of incapacitation.

D. Retribution—societal vengeance.

E. Rehabilitation—subject those convicted to education, training, and therapy with the purpose of altering an individual's behavior to conform to societal norms.

3–6. These questions require answers that are partly subjective. The purpose of the questions is to initiate class discussion concerning the various methods and make each student consider the different and occasionally competing purposes.

# CHAPTER 3

## REVIEW QUESTIONS

1. A defendant must be proved to be both the factual and legal cause of the harm. Factual causation is tested using the "but for" test. But for the defendant's act the harm would not have occurred. Legal causation focuses on the similarity between:

1. the intended result and the actual result and

2. the intended method to bring about the result and the actual cause of the result.

In many jurisdictions legal causation is also called proximate causation. An act is considered the proximate cause of a result if a reasonable person would have foreseen the result.

2. No. Before criminal liability can exist for failing to save another, a duty to aid that person must be established. In most jurisdictions people owe no duty to strangers.

3. Concurrence is a legal doctrine requiring that mens rea and the act occur together. The mental state must be the cause of setting the act into motion.

4. Failing to act when required to do so is an omission. The duty to act can be imposed in many ways, including by statute, such as the requirement to file a tax return. Although not an act in reality, an omission is treated as an act for the purposes of imposing criminal liability.

5. The four mens rea under the Model Penal Code are purposeful, knowing, reckless, and negligent. Purposeful characterizes the state of mind wherein a person has a desire to cause a specific result. Knowing is a state of mind where the actor may not desire to cause a specific result, but knows (or should know) with practical certainty that the result will occur. Reckless is similar to knowing, only a lesser risk is involved. To be reckless, an actor must be aware of a substantial and unjustified risk. To be negligent, the actor must take a substantial and unjustified risk, as with recklessness, but the act is taken without an awareness of the risk.

6. When one can be held criminally liable for the acts of another.

7. Presumptions are conclusions that judges or juries sometimes make. A presumption is rebuttable if the law permits it to be disproved. For example, a person is innocent until proven guilty. An irrebuttable presumption may not be disproved, despite the amount of evidence.

8. Yes. Under the common law, corporations, for the most part, were not liable for criminal acts. Today, this is not true. Of course, corporate liability is achieved through vicarious liability.

9. Mens rea is the state of mind that leads to the criminal act. Motive is the underlying reason for the mens rea and the criminal act. By law, prosecutors are required to prove mens rea but are not required to prove motive. As a practical matter, prosecutors often must prove motive in order to obtain a conviction.

## REVIEW PROBLEMS

1–6. Statute one defines a specific intent crime under the common law. Under the Model Penal Code the mens rea would be purposeful. This is true because the inmate must "pass beyond the borders of an institution with an intent to never return." Hence, the purpose is to never return. If an inmate does not have such a purpose, statute one has not been violated.

Statute two does not have an explicit mens rea requirement. It is probable that this statute will be read by courts as one of strict liability.

1. Spike intended to return, so Spike has a defense of lack of mens rea, as to statute one. Statute two, being

strict liability, was violated as soon as Spike passed over the boundary line of the facility. All that must be examined in strict liability cases is whether the defendant took the act freely. Spike did so in question number one.

2. Spike did not have as his purpose never returning to the facility. As such, he has a defense to statute one. To prove strict liability statutes, all that has to be proved is that the act occurred. However, the act must be voluntary. As such, he has a defense of no act against both statutes because his movement of falling outside the borders of the facility was not voluntary.

3. Spike has no defenses, as his intent to never return satisfies statute one, and his movement across the boundary line of the facility satisfies the second requirement of statute one and the requirement of statute two.

4. Again, Spike did not possess the requisite mens rea to be convicted under statute one. He also has a defense against statute two because he ended up outside the fence not by his own act, but by Ben's.

5. This question involves a problem with concurrence. Spike possessed the requisite mens rea, but it is debatable whether the act joined with the mens rea. While the mens rea did set the act into motion indirectly, there appears to be a lack of concurrence because Spike did not plan for the act to happen at that moment. However, strict liability crimes require no mens rea, and, as such, concurrence is not a problem. The issue as to statute two is whether Spike can be held accountable for passing over the boundary of the facility. He can because he enlisted Ben to throw him over the fence.

6. Spike has a defense as to statute two, but not statute one. While he did not leave the facility voluntarily, once beyond the boundary he had an obligation to return. By choosing to run, it can be assumed that he was intending to escape. However, to violate statute two, one must pass over the boundary line of the facility. In this case, he did not pass over voluntarily so he did not violate statute two.

7. Although purposeful would normally require that the defendant actually intend to cause the harm that actually resulted to the person or thing that was actually harmed, no defense exists herein because of the doctrine of transferred intent. The doctrine applies because the crime is one requiring a show of intent to cause a harm, the resulting harm was substantially similar to what she intended, and Penni's liability was not increased by the transfer.

8. Yes. Since he entered into an agreement whereby he was to supervise the trip, he had a duty to attempt to save the drowning boys. His failure to try to save the boys is an omission. His duty was created by the contract with the troop.

9. Yes. Sherri is the factual cause of the death. "But for" her act of burning her home, the worker would not have fallen from the ladder. However, she is not the legal cause of the worker's death. To be the legal cause of the death it must be shown that there is a relationship between the intended result and the actual result; that the intended result is proximate to the actual result. This cannot be shown. It is reasonable to think that the fire may spread to buildings close to Sherri's home, but it is not reasonably foreseeable that a neighbor will be storing enough explosives to cause such a tremendous blast. It is even less foreseeable that a person working on a house located a block away would be harmed by the fire.

10. Jane's defense is that she took no act. The statute makes her status as a pedophile illegal. Generally, a person's status or condition does not constitute an act and may not be made criminal. Of course, if Jane were to act on her sexual impulses, then she may be prosecuted. It is probable that this statute would be found unconstitutional, as violative of the Fifth, Eighth, and Fourteenth Amendments to the United States Constitution.

11. Section 2.10(4) of the Model Penal Code states that possession can be an act when "the possessor knowingly procured or received the thing possessed or was aware of his control thereof for a sufficient period to have been able to terminate his possession." This section includes what has traditionally been known as actual and constructive possession. Clearly, Janice can be charged with possession, since she exercised actual possession over the cocaine. Ashley, Amy, and Karen may be charged since they each exercised dominion and control over the premises if constructive possession is proved.

Amy does have a defense, because she had no knowledge that the cocaine was in the apartment, and, as such, she was not "aware of her control." Ashley also has a defense because she acted to terminate her possession. Karen, on the other hand, was a possessor because she knew of the cocaine, had adequate time to terminate the possession, and did not do so. In fact, she was the cause of Janice bringing the cocaine back into the apartment.

12. Discussion question.

13. Discussion question.

14. Discussion question.

## CHAPTER 4

### REVIEW QUESTIONS

1. First- and second-degree murder are commonly differentiated by the lack of premeditation or deliberation in second-degree murder. Normally, some fact, such as "heat of passion," works to prevent the killer from forming the requisite mens rea.

2. A felony-murder occurs when someone is killed during the course of certain named felonies, i.e., robbery or rape. Despite the lack of intent to cause a death the defendant may be liable. There must be a nexus between the homicide and the crime.

3. Traditionally, battery has been defined as an unlawful, harmful, or offensive touching of another. Assaults can either be:

    1. incomplete batteries or;

    2. intentionally putting another in fear or apprehension of an impending battery.

    The first requires an intent to batter, and no knowledge of the victim of the act is required. The second form of assault requires no intent to actually batter, only to cause the victim apprehension concerning an impending battery. Also, the second form requires knowledge by the victim, or there would be no apprehension.

4. The marital rape exception provided that men were not criminally liable for raping their wives. Additionally, men were not liable for simple assaults committed on their wives that occurred as a result of the wife not submitting to sex with her husband.

5. Catching a spouse in the act of adultery is adequate provocation to reduce the homicide to voluntary manslaughter.

6. Self-defense acts to negate liability entirely. Imperfect self-defense, however, occurs when a person is mistaken about the danger to himself and reasonably, but erroneously, believes that the force used is necessary for protection. In such cases, the defense acts to reduce a resulting homicide from murder to voluntary manslaughter.

7. Kidnapping involves asportation (movement) and false imprisonment does not.

8. Mayhem.

9. Sex with a person who is incapable of understanding the nature of sex due to mental or emotional disability is a nonforcible rape, as is so-called "statutory rape," or rape with a person under a specific age.

10. The killing of another human being with malice aforethought.

### REVIEW PROBLEMS

1. The elements of forcible rape are:

    1. sexual intercourse with

    2. another

    3. against that person's will

    4. by force or such a threat of force that resistance would have resulted in serious bodily injury.

This changes the common law in the following ways:

    1. The statute is gender neutral.

    2. It does not contain a marital rape exception.

    3. The victim is not required to resist if it is reasonable to believe that serious bodily injury or death would result.

2. First, by his own admission, Mark clearly intended to assault Sam. Further, he battered him.

Regarding the homicide, since he used a deadly weapon he could be convicted of first-degree murder. The deadly weapon doctrine could be used by Mark's jury to conclude that he intended Sam's death and, accordingly, to convict Mark of first-degree murder. If the jury believed that Mark only intended to cause Sam serious bodily injury, then they could convict him of second-degree murder. Finally, if the jury believed his story entirely (that he only intended a minor injury), then he could be convicted of manslaughter.

3. First, he may claim that he wasn't the legal cause of her death, if the jurisdiction in which Jeff is charged uses the year-and-a-day rule. His second defense would be that he wasn't the actual cause of death; that the physician who disabled the life support system was the actual cause of death.

Of course, both defenses are hinged on the question of when death occurs. If the jurisdiction uses the older respiration and heartbeat test, then he would probably be successful with the claim that he wasn't the legal cause of death in those jurisdictions that utilize the year-and-a-day rule, as her respiration did not stop until fourteen months after Jeff's act. For the same reason he would likely be successful with the claim that he was not the actual cause of death. In those jurisdictions that recognize brain death, he would probably not escape liability, as she would have been dead as of June 15, 1991. This would be true even if the state used the year-and- a-day rule, as her brain death occurred within one year and a day.

4. Of course, battery can be charged. However, most jurisdictions have either a mayhem or aggravated battery statute that would apply. For aggravated battery it would have to be shown that serious bodily injury resulted. That could be done with this set of facts. For mayhem, the lacerations to the face may not be enough, but the loss of the ear would certainly be.

5. The statute provides for three mens rea: purposeful, knowing, and reckless. Clearly, Eddie did not have as his purpose the death of Mikie. To be knowing, the Model Penal Code requires "practical certainty" that the result would occur. This cannot be proven from the facts. Finally, to be reckless it must be shown that his conduct was a "gross deviation" from a law-abiding person's standard of conduct. Again, this cannot be proven. Eddie used an insecticide that was available on the market, and there was no reason for him to suspect that there would be such a result.

6. The elements of kidnapping are:

1. The unlawful

2. taking and confinement and

3. asportation of

4. another person

5. by force or threat.

The issue that must first be resolved is whether making Tracy move from where she met the robber to the location of her car was asportation. Using the Model Penal Code approach it would not be since the move did not increase the risk to her life. The move appeared to be incidental to the robbery.

7. Discussion question.

8. Collection of revenue; regulation for health and safety, including testing for STDs; and prevention of minors from patronizing prostitutes, to name a few advantages.

9. Discussion question.

# CHAPTER 5

## REVIEW QUESTIONS

1. When one gains entry to a building using fraud there has been a constructive breaking. The concept of constructive breaking was used as a substitute for the actual breaking requirement of the common law.

2. The trespassory taking and carrying away of personal property of another with an intent to deprive the owner thereof.

3. Criminal mischief is the intentional destruction or damaging of property belonging to another.

4. Simple larceny involves only a loss of property. Embezzlement involves a violation of a trust, as well as a theft. It is important to preserve the integrity of trust relationships, such as between lawyers and their clients.

5. Racketeer Influenced and Corrupt Organizations Act. The basic elements are:

1. The defendant received money or other income

2. from a pattern of racketeering activity

3. and invested that money in an enterprise

4. that is involved in interstate commerce.

6. Fences are people who purchase stolen goods from thieves and then resell the goods for a profit. Fences commit the common-law crime of receiving stolen property. This crime is now often part of statutes that consolidate theft.

7. The Model Penal Code treats causing an explosion of a structure as arson, if purposeful. At common law, causing a structure to explode was not arson, unless part of the structure survived the explosion and then burned from the fire caused by the blast.

8. Larceny.

9. Since force was necessary to acquire the purse, the crime is robbery.

10. Forgery is the making of the false document (or the alteration of the existing document making it false) with knowledge of its false character and an intent to defraud. No act of using the document need occur. Uttering is the passing of the false document to the victim. The defendant who utters must intend to defraud, but need not have participated in making the document.

## REVIEW PROBLEMS

1. Today, arson includes the burning of any structure; under the common law, arson could only be committed on a home. Causing a building to explode was not arson until made so by statute. Also, under the common law the fire had to touch the structure and cause some damage. The Model Penal Code only requires that the fire be set, accompanied by the requisite mens rea. The Code does not require that the structure actually be touched by the flame.

2. First, the common-law definition of burglary included only dwellings; today many types of structures may be burglarized. Second, under the common law the defendant had to "break" into the dwelling. Many statutes have done away with the breaking requirement, only requiring some form of unlawful entry. Finally, the night requirement has been eliminated.

3. Two crimes have been committed: false pretenses and embezzlement. Ned's acquisition of title to the Corvette was false pretenses, as he intentionally used a false statement to convince the couple to pass title to the automobile to him.

The conversion of the trust money was embezzlement, since he took it during a trust relationship and did not intend to take it until after he had possession.

4. Criminal mischief should be charged for both the scratch by the key and the burning of the vehicle. The student should be aware that arson usually only applies to buildings, not personal property.

5. Kevin has committed larceny, as he took and carried away (asportation) personal property of another with an intent to deprive the owner of the property. His sale of the ring (and consumption of the drink) is proof of his intent. When he picked the ring up, placed it into his pocket, and then left with it, the asportation requirement was satisfied. While he also committed trespass, he did not commit a burglary. This is because one must have an intent to commit a felony when the breaking occurs. Kevin's intent was only to steal a soft drink at the time he broke the window and entered the house. In most jurisdictions, the value of cola does not rise to the level of felony-larceny. The larceny of the ring was likely a felony, but he did not form this intent until he entered the house. Of course, one practical problem that Kevin will have is proving that he did not intend to steal the ring when he entered the house. A jury could infer from the circumstances that he did possess such an intent and convict Kevin of burglary.

6. Extortion.

7. Robbery/armed robbery.

8. Discussion question.

# CHAPTER 6

## REVIEW QUESTIONS

1. Solicitation.

2. No. The United States Supreme Court held that no such right exists in the Constitution in *Bowers v. Hardwick,* 478 U.S. 186 (1986).

3. Both the federal government and the states are prohibited by the First Amendment from regulating expression, even if thought to be sexually repulsive, unless it is obscene. In *Miller v. California,* 413 U.S. 15 (1973), the test for obscenity was set out as:

    1. The average person, applying contemporary community standards, would find that the work, taken as a whole, appeals to the prurient interest and

    2. the work must depict or describe, in a patently offensive manner, sexual conduct specifically defined by the applicable state law, and

    3. the work, when taken as a whole, must lack serious literary, artistic, political, or scientific value.

4. Fighting words are those that are likely to cause an immediate breach of the peace or a violent reaction by those who hear them. Fighting words are not protected speech under the First Amendment.

5. No. While blood-alcohol tests are common, driving under the influence may be proved by field sobriety tests, videotape of the defendant at the time of arrest or immediately thereafter, or other means. Statutes provide that anyone who is unable to operate a vehicle safely, due to alcohol or drugs, is guilty of driving under the influence. Blood-alcohol levels, which are established by statute, create an irrefutable presumption of inability to operate the vehicle safely.

6. Continuing Criminal Enterprise is aimed at "drug kingpins." Its elements are:

    1. Defendant is an organizer, administrator, or other leader of

    2. a group of five or more people

    3. who are involved in a series of drug violations. Series has been defined by case law as three or more violations.

7.   1. To solicit or accept

    2. anything of value

    3. with the purpose of

    4. violating a duty or trust.

The Model Penal Code provides for bribery of public officials and in commercial situations.

8. The purpose of civil contempt is to coerce someone into future behavior. The purpose of criminal contempt is to punish someone for violating a prior court order. Any contemptuous act that occurs before a

judge is direct contempt. Acts that occur outside the presence of a court are indirect.

9. Untrue. Perjury laws apply to many documents and statements. Statutes provide that any false statement made while under oath before an authorized official is perjury. This applies to many situations, such as testifying before a legislative body or signing a document before a notary.

10.    1. Exposure of

      2. one's private parts

      3. in a public place.

11. The elements of treason as defined in 18 U.S.C. § 2381 are:

      1. A person who owes an allegiance to the United States

      2. levies war or adheres to an enemy of the United States and

      3. commits an overt act and

      4. possesses treasonable intent.

12. The Patriot Act expanded federal authority in the following ways:

      1. Federal law enforcement officers' authority to monitor e-mail and other forms of communication was expanded. Examples include treating stored voice-mail messages like e-mail, not as telephone conversations. E-mail enjoys less protection than telephone conversations.

      2. Broadening federal court authority to issue pen register and trap orders (devices used to determine the origin of electronic communications).

      3. Prior to the Patriot Act, law enforcement officers did not have to establish probable cause to obtain a court order to a telephone company to trace (using pen register/traps). Because the content of telephone conversations was not being intruded upon, law enforcement officers were only required to show that the data was "relevant to an ongoing investigation." The Patriot Act extended this procedure to obtaining a record of Web addresses a suspect visits, even though identification of a Web address also identifies content.

      4. The Patriot Act authorizes "roving wiretaps." A roving wiretap is authorization to move a wiretap from one telephone or form of communication to another in order to follow the communications of the person under surveillance.

      5. Several new crimes were created, including money laundering of cybercrime and terrorism, overseas use of fraudulent U.S. credit cards, terrorist attacks on mass transit, and harboring terrorists. It also increased the penalties for counterfeiting.

      6. The Attorney General of the United States was delegated greater authority to deport suspected alien terrorists.

      7. Law enforcement agencies were given the authority to share grand jury and wiretap information that constitutes "foreign intelligence" with intelligence agencies. Previously, this was not permitted.

## REVIEW PROBLEMS

1. Statute one is sufficiently specific. Statute two is unconstitutional, as it makes personal status a crime. The Supreme Court found a similar statute unconstitutional in *Papachristou v. City of Jacksonville*, 405 U.S. 156 (1972), because it violated the Due Process Clause by not giving people fair notice of what acts were made criminal.

2. The United States Supreme Court has held that a person may not be punished for possessing obscene materials in the home. Herb may not be convicted. It is likely that Sam will not be convicted due to lack of mens rea. The statute requires that Sam had knowledge that the magazine contained bestiality when he sold it. Since the magazine was sent to him in error, and its contents were not visible, it is unlikely that he would be convicted. Knowing under the Model Penal Code equates with "practical certainty." The fact that the magazine was entitled "Wild on the Farm" does not create a "practical certainty" that the magazine contains depictions of bestiality.

3. Individual answers may vary; however, reasons should be substantiated.

4. Originally, bribery referred to judges, but statutes extend it to commercial and public officials only.

5. Direct/criminal.

6. Indirect/civil.

7. Indirect/civil.

8. Answers may vary. Students should be encouraged to support their reasons with examples from this chapter.

9. Discussion question.

# CHAPTER 7

## REVIEW QUESTIONS

1. A principal in the first degree is the party who actually commits the crime. A principal in the second degree is present during the crime and assists the principal in the first degree. They are punished equally.

2. An accessory before the fact.

3. No. Thoughts are not criminal acts. She must take some act in furtherance of her objective for there to be an attempt.

4.    1. An agreement

2. between two or more people

3. to commit an unlawful act or a lawful act in an unlawful manner.

5. In evidence, hearsay is an out-of-court statement. As a general rule, hearsay is inadmissible. The co-conspirator exception permits statements made by co-conspirators to be admitted at trial, provided the statements were made during the conspiracy.

6. Inchoate refers to acts that have a purpose and even though that purpose is not completed, the acts are criminal.

7. Solicitation requires a request, command, or urging of another to commit a crime. No act in furtherance of the desired crime need be taken for there to be solicitation. Attempt, on the other hand, requires some act be taken in furtherance of the criminal objective. The jurisdictions differ in how far a person must go; however, mere preparation is never enough.

## REVIEW PROBLEMS

1. and 2. Abel and Baker have committed the same crimes. First, they conspired to rob the store while in prison. Second, they committed solicitation by engaging the service of Nitro. Third, attempted robbery. The acts of buying the materials necessary to construct the bomb, constructing the bomb, and going to the store are beyond preparation. Although not covered in this chapter, burglary and possession of burglary tools may have also been committed.

3. Nitro is also a conspirator. As an accessory before the fact, he is liable for attempted robbery. By providing the house, Nitro is also an accessory after the fact.

4. Attempted murder, as he possessed the requisite mens rea and committed the acts necessary to complete a murder. An interesting case that illustrates this point is *People of New York v. DLUGASH*, 41 N.Y. 2nd 725 363 NE2d 1155 (1977).

# CHAPTER 8

## REVIEW QUESTIONS

1. Affirmative defenses are special defenses. An affirmative defense is more than a denial of the alleged facts; it asserts something requiring special attention by the prosecutor. Alibi and self-defense are examples of affirmative defenses. Affirmative defenses are significant because notice to the prosecutor that one intends to rely on such a defense is often required, and often defendants bear some burden of proof, whether it be production or persuasion.

2. The elements of the M'Naghten test are:

1. At the time the act was committed

2. the defendant was suffering from a disease of the mind

3. that caused the defendant to not know either the nature and quality of his act or that the act was wrong.

The irresistible impulse test adds the following to the M'Naghten test: The defendant is not guilty if a disease of the mind causes her to be unable to control her behavior. The Model Penal Code (§ 4.01) states that a person is not responsible for her acts if she lacks substantial capacity to appreciate the wrongfulness of her act or to control her conduct.

3.    1. That the defendant was the subject of an unprovoked attack

2. posing an immediate threat of bodily harm;

3. that force was necessary to protect from the attack; and

4. the amount of force used was reasonable.

4. All people, except police officers, are required to retreat from an attack before using deadly force. Retreat is only required when it is safe.

5. Imperfect self-defense applies only to homicides and whenever a person is unable to successfully claim a perfect self-defense. There are two situations when it applies. First, whenever one uses deadly force, but is unreasonable in doing so. So long as the defendant

used the force in good faith, then the requisite mens rea for murder is absent; the crime is manslaughter, not murder. Second, whenever a defendant initiates an attack and then later justifiably uses deadly force, the crime is manslaughter.

6. Deadly force may be used when the suspect is a felon and poses a danger to the police or others.

7. Entrapment occurs when a law-enforcement officer encourages a person to engage in a crime. The objective test focuses on the conduct of the police. The subjective test focuses on the predisposition of the defendant to become involved in the crime.

8. Insane defendants may not be tried. A defendant is insane if incapable of assisting in the defense of the case.

9. Time period following the commission of a crime wherein a prosection must be initiated.

10. Legal impossibility occurs when a defendant believes his acts are illegal when they are not. No liability. Factual impossibility refers to a situation where an individual attempts to commit a crime, but the facts have made the crime not possible. Both intent and actions exist and in some circumstances the accused may have believed a crime was committed. Liability exists.

## REVIEW PROBLEMS

1. Discussion question.

2. Ira would not have a successful insanity defense in a M'Naghten jurisdiction because he understood the nature and quality of his act and knew that the act was wrong. However, he would be successful in both jurisdictions using the Model Penal Code and irresistible impulse tests.

3. Jane is likely to be successful with the defense of necessity.

4. Gary may assert an imperfect self-defense, which leaves him with manslaughter. He is not entitled to a complete self-defense because he initiated the violence.

## CHAPTER 9

## REVIEW QUESTIONS

1. A statute is vague if "men of common intelligence must necessarily guess at its meaning and differ as to its application." A statute is overboard if it criminalizes not only unprotected conduct, but conduct protected by the Constitution.

2. A bill of attainder is a legislative act punishing a person without the benefit of a judicial trial. An ex post facto law is a legislative enactment making an act criminal after it has been taken. It is also ex post facto to increase the penalty of a crime after it has occurred or to change the procedural rules (to the defendant's disadvantage) after the criminal act was taken.

3. No. Yes.

4. No.

5. Fourteenth.

6. No. Yes.

7. All are protected.

## REVIEW PROBLEMS

1. Discussion question.

2. The United States Supreme Court has upheld the right of the Amish to refrain from compulsory school attendance. In such cases a balancing between the state's interest and the First Amendment rights at issue must occur. The fact that the defendants provide education to their children is important.

3. Discussion question.

4. Discussion question.

## CHAPTER 10

## REVIEW QUESTIONS

1. To pursue justice.

2. By protecting the rights of the accused, the civil liberties of all persons are protected.

3. Confidential communications between an attorney and client may not be disclosed by an attorney without the consent of the client, nor may an attorney be compelled to testify as to those communications.

4. Rendering legal advice, appearing in court, establishing a lawyer-client relationship, and establishing legal fees.

5. Yes. Both the legal assistant code of ethics and attorney code of ethics (made applicable to legal assistants through the NALA code) require this.

6. A comprehensive set of laws, statutory or constitutional, providing that crime victims have rights, includ-

ing, the right to attend and participate in court proceedings, to submit victim impact statements to be considered in sentencing, to confer with prosecutors concerning case dispositions, to restitution and civil damages, and to be notified of the perpetrator's status once imprisoned, including parole and release decisions.

7. Force should be used with great restraint and only after discussion, negotiation, and persuasion have been found inappropriate or ineffective.

8. United States Code and Federal Rules of Criminal Procedure.

## REVIEW PROBLEMS

1. Problem requires the student to develop facts where joint representation would cause at least one defendant to be deprived of the effective assistance of counsel, such as when defenses are antagonistic.

2. Discussion question.

3. Discussion question.

4. Discussion question.

5. Discussion question.

## CHAPTER 11

### REVIEW QUESTIONS

1. Incorporation refers to extending a right found in the United States Constitution to state criminal proceedings. Only fundamental rights that are essential to the concept of ordered liberty are incorporated. This is known as selective incorporation and is current law. Total incorporation would make the entire Bill of Rights applicable against the states.

2. Nearly all of the rights contained in the Bill of Rights have been incorporated. The right to be charged by indictment has not been, as had trial by jury in civil cases.

3. All evidence that is obtained by law enforcement in an unconstitutional manner is inadmissible at trial.

4. Students are to create an answer.

5. Attenuation, independent source, and inevitable discovery.

6. Emphasizing the importance of State Constitutions with respect to individual rights and criminal procedure.

### REVIEW PROBLEMS

1. The United States Constitution is important in state prosecutions because rights contained therein have been extended to state proceedings through the Fourteenth Amendment's Due Process Clause. In addition, many of those rights that have been extended to the states have been expanded.

2. Discussion question.

3. Discussion question.

## CHAPTER 12

### REVIEW QUESTIONS

1. Prior to the Katz decision, the Fourth Amendment was viewed as protecting physical areas. Katz states that the Fourth Amendment protects people, not places. This issue is one of privacy; if a person has a reasonable expectation of privacy, then the Fourth Amendment comes into play.

2.  1. There must be probable cause to believe that the items sought will be within the area searched;

   2. probable cause to believe that the items sought are connected to criminal activity;

   3. the area searched and the items to be seized must be described with particularity;

   4. the allegations must be supported by oath or affirmation; and

5. the warrant must be issued by a neutral and detached magistrate.

3. Yes. Any area may be searched so long as the requirements for obtaining a search warrant are met, such as probable cause to believe that the evidence is in the home. The fact that the evidence is located in a third person's home is not vital.

4. The plain view doctrine is an exception to the warrant requirement. If an officer, who is in a place lawfully, sees an illegal item, it may be seized without first obtaining a warrant.

5. Curtilage is the area directly around one's home. A homeowner's property beyond his curtilage area is open field. Curtilage is protected by the Fourth Amendment, and open fields are not.

6. The Fourth Amendment requires probable cause to believe that a person committed a crime before an

arrest can be made. However, the Supreme Court announced in *Terry v. Ohio* that a limited seizure may be conducted on a lesser quantity of suspicion: the officer must have a reasonable suspicion that criminal activity is afoot. This is known as an investigatory stop. Such stops must be brief and reasonable—no longer than necessary to dispel an officer's suspicions.

To conduct a search, an officer must have probable cause and a warrant, unless an exception to the warrant requirement applies. Again, *Terry v. Ohio* recognizes that upon reasonable suspicion to believe the detainee has a weapon a limited frisk of the person's outer clothing is permitted.

7. No. There is no warrant requirement for arrests made in public. For the arrest to be valid the officer must have probable cause to believe that a crime has been committed and that the person being arrested is the guilty party. The victim's statements to the officer are sufficient to justify arrest.

8. Yes. To make an arrest in the home an arrest warrant, which inherently includes the authority to search the premises for the defendant, must be obtained unless an exception exists. No such exception exists herein.

9. No. The hot pursuit exception applies.

10. A limited, warrantless search of the premises where an arrest is made to protect against other potentially dangerous people who may be hiding.

## REVIEW PROBLEMS

1. First, it must be determined whether the detention of Tommy was valid. Yes, the detention was initially valid. The fact that he was in an alley behind a commercial establishment at 11:50 for over five minutes creates a reasonable suspicion. Under *Terry v. Ohio* the officer had the authority to conduct an investigatory stop. However, once Tommy answered the question and presented his identification, the suspicion was dispelled and the seizure should have ceased. Under this view, the subsequent searches were violative of the Fourth Amendment.

In the alternative, if the student chooses to find that reasonable suspicion has not dissipated, the second issue is: was the frisk valid? To conduct a frisk, an officer must have a reasonable suspicion that the detainee is carrying a weapon. Then, the search is limited to finding weapons in the person's outer clothing. At the point the officer frisked Tommy the quantity of suspicion of a crime being afoot had decreased and the officer had no reason to believe that Tommy was carrying a weapon. The frisk was conducted in violation of the Fourth Amendment. Since the frisk produced the evidence upon which Tommy was arrested, the arrest is invalid. Since the arrest was invalid, the search incident to arrest was invalid. Accordingly, the tools and diagram must be suppressed. There being no additional evidence, the motion to dismiss must also be granted.

2. The desk drawers may not be searched. It is not reasonable to expect stereos to be found in such a small place.

3. The closets may be searched, as stereos may be hidden there.

4. No, unless: (1) The warrant authorizes the officer to search the defendant or (2) they have a reasonable suspicion to believe he has a weapon—then they may frisk the defendant (3) they arrest the defendant and conduct a search incident to arrest.

5. They may seize the bag under the plain view rule.

6. Discussion question.

7. Discussion question.

8. Discussion question.

# CHAPTER 13

## REVIEW QUESTIONS

1. The right to remain silent; to the assistance of counsel; that counsel will be appointed if the arrestee is indigent; and that any statement made by the defendant may be used to gain a conviction. The warnings must be read any time a defendant is in custody and subjected to an interrogation.

2. The confession is suppressed.

3. Under both the Federal Wiretap Act and Fourth Amendment analysis, one party may consent, without the other's knowledge, to a third person listening to the conversation. Hence, Terry has no basis to have the statements suppressed.

4. There is no right to counsel at a lineup conducted before the adversary judicial proceeding has been initiated. But once the formal proceedings have been started, the Sixth Amendment guarantees the right to counsel.

5. No.

6. Traditional line phones may not be intercepted by the public generally. A cordless telephone uses radio waves, which may be received by any person, and, as such, it is reasoned that there is no reasonable expectation of privacy.

7. A record of who had possession of evidence from the time it was seized until it is introduced at trial.

8. Scientific testing is not testimonial, so the Fifth Amendment challenge would fail. Because the testing would require an invasion of the defendant's person, the Fourth Amendment requires that the government establish probable cause that the defendant committed the offense and that the hairs found on the rape victim belonged to the rapist. In addition, the test must be conducted in a reasonable manner. Since there is no emergency, a warrant must be obtained.

## REVIEW PROBLEMS

1. Generally, a person must be in custody and subject to interrogation before the *Miranda* warnings must be read. Tom's first statement should not be suppressed for two reasons. First, Tom was not in custody when the statement was made. Second, even if he had been, the question by the officer was spontaneous and falls into an exception to the interrogation element of *Miranda*. Accordingly, the baseball bat should not be suppressed. The second statement, concerning his motive, should be suppressed because the officer was not acting impulsively and Tom was both in custody and interrogated.

2. The motion should be denied. Court orders for surveillance implicitly authorize reasonable entries onto/into a person's premises to install the necessary equipment.

3. Because of the possibility of coercion, threat, and other abuses.

4. Discussion question.

5. Discussion question.

# CHAPTER 14

## REVIEW QUESTIONS

1. To assure the defendant's appearance at trial and to prevent danger to the public.

2. Indictments are issued by grand juries, and informations are filed by prosecutors.

3. Indictments and informations are the formal charging instruments; they begin the process and provide the defendant with notice of the charges pending against her.

4. The defendant should file a motion for a bill of particulars.

5. Pleas of nolo contendere may not be used in subsequent civil proceedings.

6. Kevin should file a motion to suppress the weapon.

7. The answer can differ, depending on whether the complaint was initially used to obtain an arrest warrant or at a preliminary hearing. In either case its purpose is the same: to establish probable cause. However, since a preliminary hearing was included in the list, the following order is most sensible: Complaint; Initial Appearance; Preliminary Hearing; Formal Charge; Arraignment; and Trial.

8. Brady requires prosecutors to disclose to defendants all exculpatory information in their possession (or which may be found through due diligence). Failure to do so is violative of the Due Process Clause.

9. When federal officials or members of the military are charged with crimes that arise out of performance of official duties.

10. The surrender of a person from one government/jurisdiction to another for prosecution.

## REVIEW PROBLEMS

1. Historically grand juries were used to shield people from arbitrary prosecutions. They were the "buffer" between the people and the government. Many argue that grand juries have lost their independence—that they are tools of prosecutors. This is particularly important, as grand juries have powers (investigative) that prosecutors do not. So the result has not been to limit governmental power, but to increase it.

2. Discussion question.

3. Discussion question.

# CHAPTER 15

## REVIEW QUESTIONS

1. The right to be at one's trial, to cross-examine government witnesses, and for the government to produce their witnesses at trial (avoid hearsay).

2. Beyond a reasonable doubt. Greater than preponderance, but less than absolute confidence of guilt. A doubt causing a reasonable or prudent person to question the guilt of the accused is a reasonable doubt.

3. The Supreme Court has not set a specific time period within which a defendant must be tried. In determining whether speedy trial has been violated the Court established four factors to be considered:

1. The length of the delay;

2. the reason for the delay;

3. whether the defendant asserted his right to a speedy trial; and

4. the prejudice caused by the delay.

4. When a jury disregards the law. Neither party may encourage a jury to nullify the law.

5. Judges decide whether prospective jurors may be dismissed for cause. Inability to be fair is cause. The parties are given a stated number of peremptory challenges to eliminate jurors for any reason, except race, etc.

6. Yes.

7. 1. The representation was extremely inadequate and

2. of actual harm.

## REVIEW PROBLEMS

1. There is no right to a jury trial in juvenile proceedings.

2. Jane is entitled to a jury trial since the crime may be punished with more than six months imprisonment.

3. Nick is entitled to a jury trial since he is being tried as an adult.

4. There is no right to a jury trial in the military.

---

## CHAPTER 16

---

## REVIEW QUESTIONS

1. The presentence investigation is conducted by the probation office of the sentencing court. The investigation gathers information about the defendant, which the judge will need for sentencing. Typically, financial, family, alcohol and drug use, prior criminal activity, employment, medical, and psychological information is gathered. This information is then put into a presentence report, which is provided to the sentencing judge.

2. Aggravating circumstances are reasons for a court to sentence a defendant higher than a presumptive sentence. Mitigating circumstances are reasons to sentence a defendant below a presumptive sentence.

3. Only final judgment may be appealed. Other decisions, which do not end the case, must wait until final judgment before they may be reviewed by an appellate court.

4. If state law provides for appeal by right then the Fourteenth Amendment's Equal Protection Clause guarantees counsel. However, if the appeal is discretionary, there is no right to counsel.

5. Habeas Corpus is a method of attacking a conviction. It is a civil remedy used to review a conviction for constitutional error.

6. No trial is perfect, and harmless errors do not lead to reversal. If an error prejudices a defendant, then the defendant must be freed or retried.

7. Yes.

8. Items a, b, and d are not inherently cruel. Flogging is unresolved. Item e is violative of the Eighth Amendment.

9. A suspended imposition of sentence occurs when a court withholds sentencing for a period of time and then dismisses the case when this period expires if the defendant complies with the conditions established by the court (i.e., no other arrests or convictions). A sentence suspended to probation is entered into the record and the defendant is released subject to conditions.

## REVIEW PROBLEMS

1. The prosecution will not be successful on appeal. To overturn the conviction would be violative of the Double Jeopardy Clause of the Fifth Amendment. The prosecutor erred by not seeking an interlocutory appeal, as most states permit interlocutory appeals of such pretrial orders.

2. Again, contrary to the final judgment, a decision concerning a defendant's competency to stand trial may be appealed immediately under the collateral order doctrine. However, failure to bring an interlocutory appeal does not waive the issue; it may be raised on appeal after judgment.

3. Discovery issues may not be appealed until after final judgment has been issued. As such, the appeal will be dismissed.

4. Fourth Amendment issues may not be raised in a habeas corpus proceeding. His petition would be dismissed at an early stage without a hearing.

## CHAPTER 1

1. Which of the following is not true about the distinction between civil and criminal law?

   A. A purpose of civil law is to compensate individuals for injuries caused by others.

   B. A purpose of criminal law is to deter future misconduct.

   C. A purpose of civil law is to punish individuals for misconduct.

   D. A purpose of criminal law is to punish individuals for misconduct.

2. A court of record is one that:

   A. Maintains a comprehensive filing system

   B. Keeps verbatim records of its hearings and trials

   C. Maintains docket sheets

   D. Is an intermediate level appellate court and above

3. Judicial Review is best defined as:

   A. A review of a trial court's actions by an appellate court

   B. The authority of a court to hear a case

   C. An evaluation of a judge's behavior by a judicial disciplinary panel

   D. The power of the judicial branch to review the actions of the executive and legislative branches

4. Separation of Powers is a phrase referring to:

   A. The division of power between the federal government and the states

   B. The division of power between the executive, legislative, and judicial branches of government

   C. The division of power between the two levels of courts: the trial and appellate

   D. The division of power between the various law enforcement agencies of the federal government

5. Which of the following best describes the responsibility of the executive branch in criminal law?

   A. The detection, investigation, and prosecution of criminals

   B. The determination of what behavior is criminal

   C. The creation of written law prohibiting behavior found to be dangerous or undesirable by society

   D. The trial of alleged criminals

6. A court of general jurisdiction has the authority to hear:

   A. All cases arising under state law, whether civil or criminal

   B. All criminal cases arising under state law

   C. All civil cases arising under state law

   D. Either all civil cases or all criminal cases arising under state law

7. The burden of proof in most civil cases is:

   A. Preponderance of the evidence

   B. Clear and convincing evidence

   C. Beyond a reasonable doubt

   D. Beyond a shadow of a doubt

8. The burden of proof in criminal cases is:

   A. Preponderance of the evidence

   B. Clear and convincing evidence

   C. Beyond a reasonable doubt

   D. Beyond a shadow of a doubt

9. T or F    Most law enforcement activities in the United States are performed by federal officers.

10. T or F    A person who commits a battery may be held liable in both civil and criminal courts.

11. T or F    The Supreme Court of the United States agrees to hear only a small percentage of the cases appealed to it.

12. T or F    Punitive damages may only be awarded in criminal cases.

13. T or F    Only the government may file criminal charges.

14. T or F    The Tenth Amendment to the United States Constitution grants certain rights to the states and reserves all others for the federal government.

15. T or F    A person injured by another's negligence may sue in tort law.

## CHAPTER 2

1. Criminal law, as a field of law, defines:
   A. The process of law enforcement
   B. The rights of those accused of criminal conduct
   C. What a crime is
   D. The procedure for defending against a criminal accusation

2. Vital to the existence of common law is the concept of:
   A. Federalism
   B. Stare Decisis
   C. Jurisdiction
   D. The Principle of Legality

3. Which of the following sources of law is not responsible for defining criminal conduct?
   A. Court rules
   B. Administrative law
   C. Statutory law
   D. Ordinances

4. The Model Penal Code:
   A. Is the penal law of the United States
   B. Is a code drafted by scholars with the hope that the states would consider its ratification
   C. Is a code drafted by the New York legislature that has been adopted by many other states
   D. Is a code drafted by scholars for use in academic settings only

5. Which of the following statements is true?
   A. The common law is the oldest form of law in the United States and may be changed only by the Constitution.
   B. The common law is the oldest form of law in the United States and may be changed by legislative command or Constitutional provision.
   C. The common law has been completely abolished in the United States.

   D. The common law may be changed by any other form of law.

6. Which of the following is the least desirable goal of criminal law?
   A. Deterrence
   B. Retribution
   C. Incapacitation
   D. Rehabilitation

7. The common law creation of crimes is inconsistent with:
   A. Modern notions of due process
   B. The Tenth Amendment to the United States Constitution
   C. The purposes of punishing criminal law violators
   D. Modern notions of precedent

8. The principle of legality requires what of the government?
   A. Notice that conduct is illegal before the conduct occurs
   B. Notice of the right to appeal after conviction
   C. Notice of the taking of property
   D. None of the above

9. What is the source of most penal law today?
   A. Constitution of the United States
   B. Constitutions of the states
   C. Federal statutes
   D. State statute and local ordinances

10. Laws created by administrative agencies are known as:
    A. Constitutions
    B. Statutes
    C. Ordinances
    D. Rules or regulations

11. T or F  The current Constitution of the United States became effective in 1865 following the Civil War.

12. T or F  Criminal law involves a delicate balancing between civil liberties and the need to protect society.

13. T or F  Statutory law is the highest form of law.

14. T or F  Ordinances are written laws of government agencies.

15. T or F  The Constitution is an important source in defining what behavior is criminal.

16. T or F  The legality principle is simply a due process concept requiring that crimes be defined before punishments are imposed.

17. T or F  Once abolished, the common law no longer serves any function.

18. T or F  The common law is the same in every state.

19. T or F  "Nullum crimen sine lege" is a Latin phrase meaning that decisions in one case should be "precedent" for future cases.

20. T or F  Administrative agencies may promulgate criminal prohibitions, but may not determine the punishment.

## CHAPTER 3

1. Mens rea is best defined as:
   A. The mental aspect of any crime
   B. The mental and physical aspects of any crime
   C. The intent to cause a specific result
   D. The intent to take a specific physical act

2. In common-law terms, a person who intended an act, but not its consequences, acted with:
   A. Specific intent
   B. General intent
   C. Transferred intent
   D. Particular intent

3. Assume John fired a gun at Pat, intending to injure her, but not kill her. However, because of his poor aim, he fatally hit her in the ear. Under the Model Penal Code, he acted:
   A. Purposefully
   B. Knowingly
   C. Negligently
   D. Recklessly

4. At trial, a conclusion that must be made by judge or jury until disproved is a(n):
   A. Inference
   B. Rebuttable presumption
   C. Irrebuttable presumption
   D. Non-final presumption

5. A State statute states that corporate officers are liable for violations of its product safety laws, even if the duty to comply with those laws is delegated to company employees. This is an example of:
   A. Strict liability
   B. Corporate liability
   C. Liability for recklessness
   D. Vicarious liability

6–10. Mark each of the following crimes as either M for *malum prohibitum* or S for *malum in se*.

6. Failing to file a required tax return

7. Murder

8. Child molestation

9. Failing to appear in court, as ordered

10. Simple battery

11. Which of the following is most true concerning general and specific intent?
   A. General intent is easier for a prosecutor to prove.
   B. Specific intent is easier for a prosecutor to prove.
   C. They are essentially the same today.
   D. General intent requires proof of the use of a weapon while specific intent does not.

12. Which of the following crimes is best described as *malum prohibitum* and *not malum in se*?
   A. Failure to file a tax return
   B. Murder
   C. Rape
   D. Burglary

13. Which of the following is *not* a generally recognized canon of statutory construction?

   A. If possible, a statute is to be construed as constitutional.

   B. Criminal law statutes are to be construed broadly to include as many people and behaviors within their grasp as possible.

   C. The plain meaning of statutes is to be enforced unless the result is absurd.

   D. In a criminal case, ambiguous language in statutes is to read in the defendant's favor.

14. John steals a controlled substance from a pharmacy for his wife who is ill. They do not have the money to purchase the drug, which was prescribed by the wife's physician. John's intention of helping his wife is best characterized as his:

   A. Mens rea

   B. Actus reus

   C. Motive

   D. Concurrence

15. Concurrence refers to:

   A. The joining of mens rea and motive

   B. The joining of motive and actus reus

   C. The joining of actus reus and harm to a victim

   D. The joining of mens rea and actus reus

16. T or F    Generally, a person may not be prosecuted for failing to save a stranger whose life is in danger.

17. T or F    Generally, only persons and not corporations may be held criminally liable.

18. T or F    Transferred intent refers to a situation in which one individual is liable for the actions of another as a result of a special relationship.

19. T or F    Every element of a crime must be proven beyond a reasonable doubt in order for a defendant to be convicted.

20. T or F    All crimes must have two basic elements: a mental element (mens rea) and a physical element (actus reus).

21. T or F    Strict liability crimes were not recognized under the common law.

22. T or F    Generally, a failure to assist a drowning person is not criminal.

23. T or F    A parent has a moral obligation, but not legal, to obtain medical help for his or her child.

24. T or F    When courts construe criminal statutes, strict liability is presumed if the statute does not specify a mens rea.

25. T or F    Corporations may be punished for crimes.

26. T or F    Specific intent under the common law most closely resembles knowing behavior under the Model Penal Code.

27. T or F    Concurrence refers to the joining of mens rea and actus reus.

28. T or F    Although a state is unlikely to do it, a person may be punished for being homeless.

29. T or F    The year-and-a-day rule is a new development, founded upon modern medical advances.

30. T or F    Motive must be proved to establish mens rea.

## CHAPTER 4

1. Felony murder, in those jurisdictions that continue to recognize the doctrine, is normally punished equally with:

   A. First-degree murder

   B. Second-degree murder

   C. Manslaughter

   D. The highest misdemeanor recognized by state law

2. If a defendant does not intend to kill, but does intend to inflict serious bodily injury, he is guilty of which of the following if the victim dies:

   A. First-degree murder

   B. Second-degree murder

   C. Voluntary manslaughter

   D. Involuntary manslaughter

3. Assume a defendant is accused of killing a person using a knife. He is tried in a jurisdiction that recognizes the deadly weapon doctrine. At trial this means:

   A. There is an irrebuttable presumption that the defendant intended to cause the victim's death.

   B. There is a rebuttable presumption that the defendant intended to cause the victim's death.

   C. The defendant may be convicted of either first-degree murder or a lower murder.

   D. The defendant may be convicted of only first-degree murder.

   E. Both A and D are correct.

   F. Both B and C are correct.

4. Which of the following are not deadly weapons for purposes of the deadly weapon doctrine?

   A. A bowling ball

   B. A shovel

   C. A rope

   D. All of the above are deadly weapons

   E. None of the above are deadly weapons

5. The primary distinction between first- and second-degree murder is the absence of _____ in second-degree murder.

   A. Willfulness

   B. Premeditation or deliberation

   C. An intent to cause the victim's death

   D. B and C

   E. All of the above

6. If a defendant has committed a homicide resulting from mutual combat with the victim, she is guilty of:

   A. First-degree murder

   B. Second-degree murder

   C. Voluntary manslaughter

   D. Reckless manslaughter

7. So-called "rape shield laws" prevent:

   A. The admission of evidence concerning a rape victim's sexual history in all circumstances

   B. The admission of evidence concerning a rape victim's sexual history in most circumstances

   C. The admission of evidence concerning the rape victim's and defendant's sexual history

   D. Defense attorneys from requiring rape victims to give details of the rape that are humiliating to the victim

8. The primary distinction between kidnapping and false imprisonment is the absence of _____ in false imprisonment.

   A. Intent to cause death or serious bodily injury

   B. Crossing a state line

   C. Asportation

   D. A ransom demand

9. *Corpus Delecti* is best defined as:

   A. The mens rea of murder

   B. The actus reus of murder

   C. The body of a crime

   D. The motive of a person for committing a crime

10. The so-called "Megan's" laws provide for:

    A. Life incarceration for sex offenders

    B. Capital punishment for sex offenders

    C. Registration of sex offenders with police agencies

    D. Fines for sex offenders

11. In the 1997 case, *Kansas v. Hendricks,* the Supreme Court held that a sex offender may be:

    A. Civilly committed after being released from prison so long as the crime for which the offender was imprisoned was "shockingly indecent"

    B. Civilly committed after being released from prison so long as the offender suffers from a mental illness that causes him or her to be a danger to others

    C. Imprisoned for life

    D. Executed

12. Under the Model Penal Code, which of the following states of mind **never** satisfies the mens rea requirement for murder?

    A. Purposeful

    B. Reckless

    C. Negligent

    D. Both B and C

13. T or F    The Supreme Court of the United States has held that the Fourteenth and Ninth Amendments to the United States Constitution protect an individual's right to commit suicide provided the individual is competent in age and mental condition.

14. T or F    At the common law, it was not rape for a husband to physically force his wife to have sex with him.

15. T or F    In most jurisdictions today, a rape conviction may not be had if a victim does not physically resist an attacker.

16. T or F    A statute that makes it a crime to "write, speak, or otherwise communicate a belief that is offensive to the ordinary member of any racial, ethnic, or religious group" is most likely violative of the First Amendment to the United States Constitution.

17. T or F    A statute that enhances the penalty for battery if the offense was "motivated by racial, ethnic, or religious animus" is most likely violative of the First Amendment to the United States Constitution.

18. T or F    Under the Model Penal Code, only "firearms, explosives, and cutting instruments" qualify to be deadly weapons for the purpose of the deadly weapon doctrine.

19. T or F    If Jane kills her husband immediately after discovering him in bed with another woman, she is guilty of second-degree murder.

20. T or F    To have sex with a woman who is unconscious is rape.

21. T or F    If Defendant hits Victim with a rock, it is not a battery because there has been no actual contact between Defendant and Victim.

22. T or F    Under modern statutes, a woman must forcibly resist a rape, or the rapist may not be convicted.

23. T or F    At common law there were two degrees of murder and two degrees of manslaughter.

24. T or F    If Defendant cuts off Victim's arm, an aggravated battery has been committed.

25. T or F    If Defendant cuts off Victim's arm, mayhem has been committed.

# CHAPTER 5

1. Arson has changed significantly from its common-law definition. All of the following, except one, represent common changes to the common law of arson. The exception has always been true. Choose the exception.

   A. It is arson to burn an outhouse.

   B. It is arson to cause a dwelling to explode.

   C. A homeowner may be convicted of burning his or her own property, if done with an intent to collect insurance money.

   D. It is arson to burn a business.

2. Which of the following is not true?

   A. Common-law burglary could only be committed at night.

   B. Common-law burglary could only be committed in a dwelling.

   C. Common-law burglary required an actual breaking and entry into the structure.

   D. Common-law burglary required either an actual or constructive breaking into the structure.

3. A lawyer who steals a client's trust fund has committed:

   A. Larceny

   B. Embezzlement

   C. Conversion

   D. Trust larceny

4. Under the common law it would not have been larceny to steal which of the following?

   A. Stereo

   B. Stock certificate

   C. Automobile

   D. Purse

5. To be prosecuted under the federal RICO statute a "pattern of racketeering activity" must be proved. A pattern is:

   A. Two or more predicate acts

   B. Three or more predicate acts

   C. Four or more predicate acts

   D. None of the above

6. Which of the following is not true about federal RICO?

   A. It has both civil and criminal components.

   B. Its purpose is to thwart organized crime.

   C. Forfeiture may result from a RICO conviction.

   D. All individuals engaged in fraud are subject to its punishment.

7. Larry learns that Nancy and Frank are having an affair. He contacts the two, threatening to expose the relationship to their respective spouses unless they pay him $5,000.00. Larry is guilty of:

    A. Larceny

    B. Extortion

    C. Bribery

    D. Embezzlement

8. The mens rea element of receiving stolen property has two aspects. First, there must be an intent to deprive the owner of the property. Second, the prosecution must prove:

    A. Actual knowledge that the property was stolen

    B. Actual knowledge is not dispositive; so long as a reasonable person would have known the property was stolen, the crime has been committed

    C. Neither A nor B

    D. Both A and B

9. Criminal mischief commonly refers to what actus reus?

    A. Disturbing others

    B. Juvenile misdemeanors

    C. Destruction of property

    D. None of the above

10. Which of the following crimes is not included in the Model Penal Code's Consolidated Theft Statute?

    A. Larceny

    B. Robbery

    C. Extortion

    D. Embezzlement

11. "Fences" commonly commit what crime?

    A. Extortion

    B. Receiving stolen property

    C. False pretenses

    D. Larceny

12. T or F    Asportation refers to the mens rea element of the theft crimes.

13. T or F    Embezzlement of money belonging to a federally insured banking institution is both a federal and state crime.

14. T or F    The purpose of RICO is to thwart the interstate transportation of minors for illegal purposes.

15. T or F    Opening an unlocked door and stepping into a house constitutes a "breaking" for purposes of burglary.

16. T or F    Walking through an open door constitutes a "breaking" for purposes of burglary.

17. T or F    Under the Model Penal Code a defendant who is charged with larceny may be convicted of embezzlement at trial.

18. T or F    A person who has lost property to a theft crime must choose between pursuing the criminal remedy or the civil remedy.

19. T or F    Under the common law, burglary could only occur at night.

20. T or F    Burglary is a specific intent crime.

21. T or F    Extortion is commonly known as blackmail.

22. T or F    Sidney leaves her laptop computer in a study carrel at the university library while she uses the restroom. Carmen takes the computer during this time with the intention of keeping it. Carmen has committed a robbery.

23. T or F    Harry Homeowner hires Ellie Electrician to make some repairs in his home. While working on the wiring in the basement, Ellie found and pocketed a ring that was lying on a table. Ellie has committed a burglary.

24. T or F    RICO is a state statute that enhances the penalty for mail fraud.

25. T or F    At the common law, malice was the mens rea of arson.

## CHAPTER 6

1. *Miller v. California*, 413 U.S. 15 (1973), changed the law of obscenity. One element of the prior obscenity test required that the material be "utterly without redeeming social value." This was changed by *Miller* to:

    A. Shocking to reasonable persons

    B. Lacking in serious literary, artistic, political, or scientific value

    C. Lacking in any literary, artistic, political, or scientific value

    D. None of these

2. *Miller v. California*, 413 U.S. 15 (1973), had this effect on obscenity law.

   A. It further limited the authority of the government to regulate sexual materials.

   B. It increased the authority of the government to regulate sexual materials.

   C. While it changed the test used to determine if a material is subject to regulation, it neither increased nor decreased the authority of the government.

   D. It declared that only sexually explicit materials involving children may be regulated.

3. A statute that makes it a crime to be addicted to drugs:

   A. Is constitutional

   B. Is unconstitutional, as it violates the Fourteenth Amendment's Due Process Clause and the Eighth Amendment's Cruel and Unusual Punishment Clause

   C. Is unconstitutional, as it violates the First Amendment's Free Speech Clause

   D. Is unconstitutional, as it violates the Fourteenth Amendment's Equal Protection Clause

4. Which of the following is true?

   A. Prostitution is illegal in the United States by act of the Congress of the United States.

   B. Prostitution has been made illegal by the legislatures of every state in the union.

   C. Prostitution has been made illegal by most state legislatures.

   D. None of the above.

5. The federal drug "kingpin" statute is also known as:

   A. RICO, or Racketeering Influenced Corrupt Organizations Act

   B. Drug Prevention and Control Act

   C. Controlled Substances Prevention and Control Act

   D. CCE, or Continuing Criminal Enterprise Act

6. Which of the following is not an element of the federal Continuing Criminal Enterprise Act (CCE)?

   A. The defendant is an administrator, organizer, or other leader of

   B. A group of five or more people

   C. Who are involved in a series of drug crimes

   D. Involving international transportation of drugs.

7. Samra is ordered by a court to discontinue striking her employer by July 3. She refused to comply and appeared before the judge on July 5. After a stern lecture from the judge she agreed to return to work. However, the judge believes that she should be punished for her behavior. What offense has she committed, if any?

   A. Indirect criminal contempt

   B. Direct criminal contempt

   C. Civil contempt

   D. Obstruction of justice

8. John refuses to pay his court-ordered child support. The judge orders him jailed until he complies. Under which of the following does the judge find his authority to order John committed?

   A. Civil contempt

   B. Indirect criminal contempt

   C. Direct criminal contempt

   D. None of the above

9. The Model Penal Code contains a crime: failure to disperse. Under this law an officer may order two or more people to disperse, provided:

   A. The assembly is likely to cause substantial harm, serious inconvenience, annoyance, or alarm to others

   B. The assembly has caused property damage or personal injury

   C. The assembly has congregated to listen to a speaker who is disparaging to the government

   D. The officer believes the assembly may become riotous

10. Which of the following statements is not protected by the First Amendment?

    A. I believe and encourage that when the new year comes all minorities should rise against the government!

    B. I just raped your wife!

    C. You are a worthless, no-good, asshole!

    D. None of the above.

11. T or F     Mature, consenting adults may engage in homosexual conduct in the United States without interference of the government.

12. T or F     Prostitution is a crime throughout the entire United States.

13. T or F     The definition of "obscenity" varies from community to community.

14. T or F    States have a greater authority to regulate sexually explicit materials when involving children than when involving adults.

15. T or F    The First Amendment protects one's right to read and distribute sexually explicit materials, provided they are not "obscene."

16. T or F    Panhandling is protected expression under the First Amendment.

17. T or F    Nude dancing has been held obscene and not protected by the First Amendment.

18. T or F    A person who lies when testifying before a grand jury has committed subordination of perjury.

19. T or F    The federal Communications Decency Act of 1996 was invalidated because it violated the First Amendment's Free Speech Clause.

20. T or F    A statute that prohibits the possession of an item that is designed for, or primarily intended for, illegal drug use is too vague to survive federal Constitutional scrutiny.

# CHAPTER 7

1. Bill has been appointed conservator for his mother. His sister, Marge, devised a scheme to steal their dear old mother's savings. Marge presented the plan to Bill and encouraged him to steal the money. He did so and split the proceeds with Marge. Marge is best described as a(n):

   A. Principal in the first degree

   B. Principal in the second degree

   C. Accessory before the fact

   D. Accessory after the fact

2. Bill has been appointed conservator for his mother. His sister, Marge, devised a scheme to steal their dear old mother's savings. Marge presented the plan to Bill, and he agreed to proceed. Bill and Marge went to Mother's bank and Bill used his status as conservator to gain access to Mother's safe deposit box. While Marge waited outside with the bank officer, Bill removed all the money, jewels, and stock certificates in the safe box. Later the two split the contents. Marge is best described as a(n):

   A. Principal in the first degree

   B. Principal in the second degree

   C. Accessory before the fact

   D. Accessory after the fact

3. Today, nearly every jurisdiction punishes:

   A. All principals and accessories equally

   B. Principals equally accessories equally, but principals differently from accessories

   C. All principals and accessories before the fact equally; accessories after the fact different from all others

   D. All four types of principals and accessories differently

4. At common law, the mens rea of attempt was:

   A. Specific intent crime

   B. General intent crime

   C. Either specific or general intent depending on the intended crime

   D. Strict liability

5. Under the Model Penal Code, the mens rea of attempt is:

   A. Purposeful

   B. Knowing

   C. Negligent

   D. A and B

   E. A, B, and C

6. If a person takes an action believing it to be illegal, she:

   A. Is criminally liable

   B. Is not criminally liable

   C. Is criminally liable if the act is later declared illegal

   D. Is criminally liable if property damage or personal injury results

7. Nancy decides to steal from her employer, Ahmad. As she reaches into the cash register Ahmad enters the room. Nancy ceases and does not try again. However, much to her surprise, Ahmad had a security camera observing the cash register. He turned the tape over to the district attorney, who has charged Nancy with attempted theft. Nancy's

defense is abandonment. Which of the following should be the result?

A. Conviction

B. Acquittal

8. The "Wharton's Rule" would prevent two people from being charged with conspiracy to commit which of the following crimes?

A. Murder

B. Larceny

C. Rape

D. Gambling

9. Which of the following is not a test used to determine if an act is close enough to completion to permit an attempt conviction?

A. Final step test

B. Proximity test

C. Res ipsa loquitur test

D. Substantial step test

10. At common law, a person who helped a fugitive from justice hide from law enforcement was guilty of being:

A. An accessory before the fact

B. An accessory after the fact

C. A principal in the first degree

D. Both B and C

11. T or F    Winston's good faith, but incorrect belief that he has a right to smoke marijuana at home is a defense to the charge of possession and use of the substance.

12. T or F    A crime must be completed in order to convict one defendant of soliciting the aid of another defendant in the commission of the crime.

13. T or F    The Model Penal Code prohibits the use of withdrawal as a defense to conspiracy.

14. T or F    Prosecutors seldom file conspiracy charges because they are at a disadvantage in conspiracy cases.

15. T or F    Mere mental planning to commit a crime is insufficient to prove attempt.

16. T or F    Legal impossibility is a valid defense, while factual impossibility is not.

17. T or F    The objective of a conspiracy must be fulfilled before the parties can be charged with conspiracy.

18. T or F    Co-conspirators must be tried together.

19. T or F    Manuel hired Tera to kill his boss. The two have been charged with conspiracy to murder. The actus reus of the crime is the act of attempting to kill the boss.

20. T or F    Inchoate crimes refers to crimes involving more than one criminal.

## CHAPTER 8

1. Affirmative defenses are different from other defenses because:

A. They require the defendant to testify in his own behalf

B. The defendant must plead such defenses prior to trial

C. The prosecution must disprove such defenses at a hearing prior to trial or the case will be dismissed

D. They require expert proof

2. The test for insanity that requires a defendant to show that he did not understand the nature and quality of his act or that his act was wrong is the:

A. M'Naghten

B. Durham

C. Diminished capacity

D. Res ipsa loquitor

3. The Model Penal Code test for insanity is _____ than the M'Naghten test.

A. More narrow (less defendants will be successful)

B. Broader (more defendants will be successful)

C. Neither A nor B

4. Aaron mistakenly believed that Bob was attempting to kill him. Bob intended Aaron no harm. In defense, Aaron killed Bob. The jury decides that Aaron's belief is genuine, but unreasonable. Which of the following verdicts should be delivered?

A. Not guilty

B. Guilty of first-degree murder

C. Guilty of second-degree murder

D. Guilty of manslaughter

5. Under the Model Penal Code, a person may:

   A. Resist an unlawful arrest

   B. Resist an unlawful arrest, unless the officer making the arrest is fully uniformed

   C. Not resist an unlawful arrest

   D. Resist an unlawful arrest, but never use deadly force against an arresting officer

6. At common law citizens were privileged to make arrests for:

   A. All felonies and misdemeanors when the citizen had probable cause to believe the person arrested committed the crime

   B. All felonies and those misdemeanors that amounted to breaches of the peace and were observed by the arresting citizen

   C. Only felonies

   D. Citizens were not privileged to make arrests at the common law

7. At common law it was:

   A. Irrebuttably presumed that a person under the age of fourteen was incapable of criminal conduct

   B. Irrebuttably presumed that a person under the age of seven was incapable of criminal conduct

   C. Rebuttably presumed that a person under the age of seven was incapable of criminal conduct

   D. Rebuttably presumed that all minors were incapable of criminal conduct

8. The key to the subjective test for entrapment is:

   A. The conduct of the law-enforcement officers

   B. The defendant's criminal history

   C. The predisposition of the defendant

   D. Both B and C

   E. All of the above

9. Which of the following statements best describes the objective test for entrapment?

   A. It is entrapment if the conduct of the police creates a substantial risk that the offense will be committed by a person normally not ready to commit it.

   B. It is entrapment if the defendant's predisposition is not such that he was waiting for the opportunity to commit the crime.

   C. It is entrapment if the defendant has no criminal record when the police make the offer that induces the defendant to become engaged in a crime.

   D. Both A and B.

10. The time that a defendant is a fugitive normally _____ the statute of limitation.

    A. Has no affect on

    B. Tolls

    C. Tolls, unless the defendant's location is known to the police

    D. Moots

11. T or F    When using self-defense, deadly force may only be used to protect against deadly force.

12. T or F    A prosecutor must assert all affirmative defenses before trial begins.

13. T or F    The M'Naghten test for insanity is also known as the right/wrong test.

14. T or F    The Durham test for insanity is the most commonly used test in the United States.

15. T or F    In the federal system and in many states, a defendant must put the government on notice that he or she intends to seek an acquittal due to insanity at trial.

16. T or F    Ordinarily, a person who is found "not guilty by reason of insanity" is committed to a mental institution until he or she is no longer dangerous.

17. T or F    The guilty but mentally ill verdict requires that a defendant receive mental health treatment while serving his or her sentence.

18. T or F    At common law, children ten and under were legally incapable of forming the requisite mens rea to be convicted of crimes.

19. T or F    In proving entrapment, evidence of criminal history is more important to the objective test than to the subjective test.

20. T or F    The objective of the juvenile justice system is different (reformation) from that of the adult criminal justice system (punishment).

# CHAPTER 9

1. In *Graham v. Connor,* 490 U.S. 386 (1989), the United States Supreme Court held that all excessive force claims against law enforcement officers should be analyzed under:

   A. A Fourth Amendment reasonableness standard

   B. A Fourteenth Amendment due process standard

   C. An Eighth Amendment cruel and unusual standard

   D. Either A or B, depending on the facts of the case

2. As a witness, which form of immunity is the best?

   A. Transactional

   B. Derivative use

   C. Involvement

3. Which of the following is ex post facto?

   A. Stacey commits a crime on June l. On June 15 state legislature declares her guilty.

   B. Stacey commits a crime on June l. On June 15 state legislature increases the penalty for her crime and applies it retroactively.

   C. Stacey commits a crime on June l. On June 15 state legislature orders that she be tried by that body, rather than a court.

   D. Both A and C.

4. A bill of attainder is:

   A. A court order for someone to appear

   B. A court order to law enforcement to arrest someone and bring that person before the court

   C. A legislative act punishing a person without trial

   D. An act that increases the punishment for a crime after it has occurred

5. The First Amendment protected Gregory Johnson's burning of the United States flag because:

   A. It was expressive conduct

   B. It was political conduct

   C. It communicated a message

   D. None of the above

   E. All of the above

6. Which of the following abortion-related laws is unconstitutional?

   A. A statute requiring minors to obtain parental or judicial consent for the procedure

   B. A statute requiring a wife to notify her husband before undergoing the procedure

   C. A statute requiring a woman to wait twenty-four hours before undergoing the procedure, assuming no medical emergency exists

   D. A statute requiring that information concerning abortion be provided to a woman before undergoing the procedure

7. Quentin was tried for robbery. The jury returned a verdict of guilty, but the judge set aside that verdict and entered a not guilty verdict. The government has appealed, seeking reinstatement of the jury verdict. Which of the following statements concerning the appeal and the Fifth Amendment's Double Jeopardy Clause is most true?

   A. It would violate the Double Jeopardy Clause for the appellate court to reinstate the verdict.

   B. It would violate the Double Jeopardy Clause for the appellate court to reinstate the verdict, but it may order a new trial.

   C. It would not violate the Double Jeopardy Clause for the appellate court to reinstate the verdict.

   D. None of the above are correct.

8. Quentin was tried for robbery. The jury returned a verdict of not guilty and the government has filed an appeal. In that appeal the government alleges that the judge committed "substantial and harmful errors prejudicial to the government. These errors caused the government's case to fail before the jury." The government is seeking a reversal of the acquittal and a new trial. Assuming the judge did commit such errors, which of the following is most true concerning the Double Jeopardy Clause and the appeal?

   A. It would violate the Double Jeopardy Clause for the appellate court to order a new trial.

   B. It would violate the Double Jeopardy Clause for the appellate court to order a new trial unless it can be shown that the trial judge's errors rise to the level of creating a manifest necessity for a new trial.

C. It would not violate the Double Jeopardy Clause for the appellate court to correct the trial judge's errors by ordering a new trial.

D. None of the above are correct.

9. T or F    A statute that enhances a penalty for a crime because it was committed with racial animus is violative of the First Amendment's Free Speech Clause.

10. T or F    A statute that makes it a crime to post messages containing racially hateful content on the Internet is violative of the First Amendment's Free Speech Clause.

11. T or F    While a state may increase civil liberties protections beyond what is provided by the United States Constitution, it may not lessen those provided by the United States Constitution.

12. T or F    The government may prohibit religious beliefs that are disrespectful or hateful of others.

13. T or F    Racially derogatory statements directed at individuals may be punished.

14. T or F    Racial motivation for committing crimes, such as battery, may be used to enhance a sentence.

15. T or F    A statute prohibiting interracial marriage is violative of the constitutional right to privacy.

16. T or F    The Fourth Amendment to the Constitution of the United States expressly protects privacy rights.

17. T or F    All religious conduct is protected by the First Amendment.

18. T or F    The First Amendment protection of speech includes other forms of expression.

19. T or F    Before a witness may be ordered to testify to a subject that may incriminate the witness, transactional immunity must be provided.

20. T or F    A person is not competent to stand trial if she is incapable of assisting her attorney in preparing a defense.

## CHAPTER 10

1. T or F    Factual guilt is the same as legal guilt.

2. T or F    Under the International Chiefs of Police Code of Conduct, police officers are expected to attempt to obtain maximum public cooperation when enforcing the laws.

3. T or F    A *nolle prosequi* is a decision by a police officer not to arrest an alleged criminal.

4. T or F    Defense attorneys have an ethical obligation to defend their clients zealously, even if that includes immoral and illegal conduct.

5. T or F    Legal assistants may not represent criminal defendants in court.

6. T or F    The Constitutional mission of the prosecutor is to seek justice.

7. T or F    Generally, judges are not personally liable for injuries resulting from judicial decisions.

8. T or F    Generally, police officers are shielded by judicial immunity when enforcing court orders.

9. A *nolle prosequi* is:

A. A police refusal to arrest a suspect

B. A prosecutor's decision to not file charges against an individual

C. A prosecutor's decision to seek the death penalty

D. A prosecutor's decision to file a motion to suppress evidence

10. Which of the following is not required to prove a discriminatory prosecution in violation of the Fourteenth Amendment?

A. Other people similarly situated were not prosecuted.

B. The prosecutor intentionally singled the defendant out for prosecution.

C. The prosecutor personally knows the defendant.

D. The defendant's selection was based upon an arbitrary classification or unjustified standard.

11. Which justice model discussed in the text does the United States adhere to?

    A. Due Process

    B. Crime Control

    C. Efficiency Control

    D. Community Protection

12. Which of the following best describes the U.S. adversarial system?

    A. The parties work together in an attempt to discover the truth under the supervision of a judge.

    B. The parties work together in an attempt to discover the truth with the judge only becoming involved when a problem surfaces.

    C. The parties are competing and the judge plays the role of passive referee.

    D. The parties are competing and the judge plays the role of active referee.

13. The legal victim in criminal cases is:

    A. The person injured

    B. The government

    C. There is no legal victim

14. By 1987, how many states had enacted victim's rights legislation?

    A. 13

    B. 27

    C. 44

    D. 50

15. While executing a lawfully issued arrest warrant, a police officer is shielded by:

    A. Absolute immunity

    B. Qualified immunity

    C. No immunity

## CHAPTER 11

1. Which of the following statements best describes the doctrine of selective incorporation?

    A. All rights contained in the Bill of Rights are incorporated by the Fourteenth Amendment and applicable against the states.

    B. All rights deemed fundamental and essential to an ordered liberty are incorporated by the Fourteenth Amendment and applicable against the states.

    C. Only those rights recognized under the Fifth Amendment's Due Process Clause are incorporated by the Fourteenth Amendment and applicable against the states.

    D. Only those rights recognized as fundamental at the time the Fourteenth Amendment was adopted are incorporated and applicable against the states.

2. The Constitution expressly provides for the exclusionary rule in:

    A. The Fourth Amendment

    B. The Fifth and Fourteenth Amendments

    C. The Eighth Amendment

    D. None of the above

3. Which of the following is not an exception to the fruit of the poisonous tree doctrine?

    A. Independent source for the evidence.

    B. The evidence would have been inevitably discovered.

    C. The evidence is of marginal incriminating character.

    D. The evidence has no causal connection between the primary evidence and the derivative evidence.

4. Which of the following rights has not been incorporated?

    A. To be indicted by a grand jury

    B. To be tried by a jury of one's peers

    C. To have a speedy trial

    D. To be free from "unreasonable" searches and seizures

5. The exclusionary rule:

    A. Prohibits the admission of evidence at trial that was obtained by law enforcement illegally

    B. Prohibits the admission of evidence at trial that was obtained by a private citizen illegally and then surrendered to law enforcement

    C. Prohibits the admission of evidence at trial that was obtained by law enforcement in violation of the Fourth Amendment only

    D. Both A and B

6. Which of the following is most accurate concerning the affect the exclusionary rule has on prosecutions?

   A. Between .6% and 2.4% of cases not prosecuted and unsuccessfully prosecuted can be attributed to the rule.

   B. Between 3.5% and 7.6% of cases not prosecuted and unsuccessfully prosecuted can be attributed to the rule.

   C. Between 15.8% and 20.6% of cases not prosecuted and unsuccessfully prosecuted can be attributed to the rule.

   D. Between 30.5% and 50% of cases not prosecuted and unsuccessfully prosecuted can be attributed to the rule.

7. In *Mapp v. Ohio* (1961) the Supreme Court of the United States held that under the Fourth Amendment:

   A. Illegally obtained evidence is inadmissible in criminal trials in state courts

   B. Illegally obtained evidence is inadmissible in criminal trials in federal courts, but admissible in criminal trials in state courts

   C. Illegally obtained evidence is admissible in criminal trials in both federal and state courts

   D. Illegally obtained evidence may be admitted in criminal trials in both federal and state courts if the government can show good cause

8. Fred and Samantha have been neighbors for years. Fred, a dentist, dislikes Samantha, a lawyer. Fred forced entry to Samantha's house while she was on vacation in order to prove to his neighbors that Samantha was a drug user. Once inside, Fred discovered large amounts of cocaine. He took the drugs to the police where he told his story. Later, Fred was charged with trespass and Samantha was charged with possession of cocaine. Samantha filed a motion to dismiss, asserting that Fred violated the Fourth Amendment in searching her home. Which of the following outcomes is most likely?

   A. The motion will be granted if she can show that Fred is convicted of trespass.

   B. The motion will be granted regardless of whether Fred is convicted.

   C. The motion will be denied.

9. T or F    In *United States v. Leon* (1984) the Supreme Court of the United States held that the exclusionary rule does not apply in pretrial suppression hearings.

10. T or F    Every right found in the Bill of Rights has been incorporated.

11. T or F    Approximately half of the criminal prosecutions in the United States occur in state courts, and the remainder take place in the federal court.

12. T or F    The exclusionary rule applies only in federal courts.

13. T or F    Today, the United States Constitution plays a greater role in criminal procedure than it did fifty years ago.

14. T or F    The exclusionary rule applies in grand jury proceedings.

15. T or F    The exclusionary rule applies at sentencing.

# CHAPTER 12

1. The "Leon" exception to the warrant requirement allows:

   A. Officers to conduct a warrantless search if they have probable cause and an exigent circumstance exists

   B. The admission of evidence seized pursuant to an invalid warrant executed in good faith by law enforcement

   C. The admission of evidence seized pursuant to an invalid warrant if executed by law enforcement within twenty-four hours of its issuance

   D. The admission of evidence seized pursuant to a warrantless and invalid search, provided the police had a good faith belief that probable cause existed

2. One party may consent to the search of another's area, provided:

   A. The two share access, control, and use of the property

   B. The two are both listed on a lease or deed to the property

   C. The two are married

   D. None of the above

3. As a search incident to arrest, an officer may:
   A. Search only the defendant's person
   B. Search the defendant and all areas within the defendant's immediate control
   C. Search the defendant and any person with the defendant at the time of arrest
   D. Search the defendant, those areas within his immediate control, and any property owned by the defendant

4. The open fields doctrine:
   A. Extended Fourth Amendment protection to those fields adjacent to a person's home
   B. Extended Fourth Amendment protection to all fields
   C. Limited Fourth Amendment protection to only a person's home and none of the area surrounding the home
   D. Limited Fourth Amendment protection to only the area immediately around a person's home

5. Before a "Terry" investigatory stop may be made an officer must:
   A. Have a warrant
   B. Have probable cause to believe the person committed a crime
   C. Have a reasonable suspicion that criminal activity is afoot
   D. Have two witnesses who will testify that the person stopped has committed a crime

6. A protective sweep is a lawful and warrantless:
   A. Search of the premises where a defendant is arrested for the limited purpose of determining whether another potentially dangerous person is present
   B. Search of the persons of all people present where an arrest is made
   C. Search of a neighborhood or other area where a fleeing criminal is reasonably believed to be
   D. None of the above

7. In what way did *Katz v. United States* change the law of search and seizure?
   A. The probable cause definition was changed so that reasonable suspicions justify search warrants.
   B. The Fourth Amendment was held to protect people, not places.
   C. The Fourth Amendment was held inapplicable to curtilage.

D. *Katz* has no effect on Fourth Amendment law.

8. An officer must knock and announce himself before entering a person's home to execute a warrant unless:
   A. The officer's life would be endangered by so doing
   B. A third person's life would be endangered by so doing
   C. Such action would permit those inside to destroy evidence
   D. All of the above
   E. None of the above

9. In determining whether a defendant's consent to search was valid, which of the following factors are considered by a reviewing court?
   A. The age and intelligence of the suspect
   B. The length of detention
   C. Neither A nor B is considered
   D. Both A and B are considered

10. When issuing a warrant, a court may consider:
    A. All credible evidence presented, regardless of whether it is admissible at trial
    B. All credible evidence that is admissible at trial
    C. All credible evidence that is reasonably likely to be admissible at trial
    D. All evidence, regardless of admissibility at trial or credibility

11. T or F    A statute authorizing the local prosecutor to issue arrest and search warrants violates the Fourth Amendment.

12. T or F    A police officer may order the driver of a lawfully stopped automobile out of the car during the stop without probable cause to believe the driver is concealing contraband or is a threat to the officer.

13. T or F    A police officer may order the occupant (not the driver) of a lawfully stopped automobile out of the car during the stop without probable cause to believe the occupant is concealing contraband or is a threat to the officer.

14. T or F    A police officer may conduct a warrantless search of an automobile so long as probable cause exists to believe the evidence sought will be found in the automobile.

15. T or F    A police officer may conduct a warrantless search of the passenger area of an automobile if probable cause exists to believe contraband will be found in a box in the trunk.

16. T or F    It is violative of the Fourteenth Amendment for police to include ethnicity or skin color as a factor in profiles.

17. T or F    Before the police may have a dog sniff a package in search of drugs, probable cause to believe the drugs will be found in the package must exist.

18. T or F    A magistrate may consider hearsay evidence when determining whether or not to issue a warrant.

19. T or F    There is no constitutional requirement that a warrant be obtained to conduct an arrest in a public place.

20. T or F    Once a valid Terry investigatory stop is made, an officer may conduct a limited frisk of the detainee.

21. T or F    An officer may search an automobile any time a lawful stop has been made.

22. T or F    Unless a search warrant provides otherwise, search warrants are to be executed during the day.

23. T or F    A defendant who is obtained illegally by law enforcement (i.e., kidnapped) must be excluded from trial (released).

24. T or F    The plain view doctrine permits a police officer to arrest any person who commits a misdemeanor in the officer's presence.

25. T or F    A Terry frisk is limited to the detainees' outer clothing and pockets.

# CHAPTER 13

1. The right to counsel found in the *Miranda v. Arizona* case is founded upon:

   A. The Fifth Amendment right to be free from self-incrimination

   B. The Sixth Amendment right to counsel

   C. The Due Process Clauses of the Fifth and Fourteenth Amendments

   D. The Equal Protection Clause of the Fourteenth Amendment

   E. None of the above

   F. All of the above

2. A defendant must be read the *Miranda* warnings whenever he:

   A. Is in custody

   B. Is in custody and subject to interrogation

   C. Is subject to interrogation, regardless of custody

   D. None of the above

3. Jeff has been arrested. He was mirandized and requested to see his lawyer. After his attorney left the jail, the police questioned Jeff concerning the crime. During the questioning Jeff made incriminating admissions. Those admissions:

   A. Are admissible, since the police respected Jeff's request to consult with his attorney

   B. Are inadmissible, because Jeff was not mirandized again

   C. Are inadmissible, because his counsel was not present

   D. Are inadmissible, because once a person asserts his/her right to have counsel present the police may never again speak to the defendant

4. A violation of the *Miranda* decision results in:

   A. The release of the defendant

   B. The inadmissibility of any statements made

   C. The exclusion of the responsible officer from trial

   D. None of the above

5. A coerced confession should be excluded from trial. If a coerced confession is admitted:

   A. The appellate court will automatically reverse the conviction.

   B. The appellate court will reverse unless the prosecution can show, by a preponderance of the evidence, that the error was harmless.

   C. The appellate court will reverse unless the prosecution can show, by clear and convincing evidence, that the error was harmless.

   D. The appellate court will reverse unless the prosecution can show, beyond a reasonable doubt, that the error was harmless.

6. In which of the following situations does the Fourth Amendment not apply?

   A. Police have attached a bug to the inside of a person's car and eavesdrop on conversations between the driver and an occupant.

   B. Police use a radio device to eavesdrop on a conversation between two people using a cordless telephone.

   C. Police use a bugging device to eavesdrop on a conversation between two people using traditional telephones.

   D. Police put a glass to a wall in an apartment and eavesdrop on a conversation in the adjoining room.

   E. None of the above.

7. At which of the following is there no right to counsel?

   A. A fingerprinting session

   B. The taking of blood

   C. The taking of a hair sample

   D. None of the above

   E. All of the above

8. The process of seizing evidence, storing it, recording its movements and uses, and producing it for trial is known as:

   A. Evidence tagging

   B. Chain-of-custody/preservation

   C. Legal recording

   D. Securing evidence

9. Which of the following best describes the test used to determine if a person is in "custody" for *Miranda* purposes?

   A. The suspect has been "formally arrested" under the standard procedures of the police department.

   B. The suspect has been moved to a police station or detention facility.

   C. The suspect believes he is not free to leave.

   D. The suspect possesses a reasonable belief that he is not free.

10. Which of the following best describes the impact on appeal of allowing an involuntary confession to be admitted at trial?

    A. Automatic reversal of the case

    B. Reversal if the defendant can prove that she was harmed by the evidence

    C. Reversal unless the government can establish that harm did not occur

    D. It is not an issue for appeal, as the decision of the trial judge is not reviewable

11. T or F    Once an arrested suspect demands to consult an attorney, any interrogation by police after the suspect has met with the attorney must occur with the attorney present.

12. T or F    A defendant has the right to have polygraph results admitted at trial even if the government objects.

13. T or F    The polygraph exam is scientifically accepted and, accordingly, the results of polygraph exams are admissible in most courts.

14. T or F    Title III of the Omnibus Crime Control Act requires the registration of all firearms sold in the United States.

15. T or F    Once criminal charges have been filed, the Sixth Amendment's Counsel Clause provides the same protections as does the Fifth Amendment's Self-Incrimination Clause as interpreted in *Miranda*.

16. T or F    A defendant has a right to a lineup that is not unfairly suggestive of guilt.

17. T or F    One-man showups are so suggestive of guilt that they are inherently unconstitutional and may never be admitted at trial.

18. T or F    A suspect has a right to counsel at photograph identification sessions.

19. T or F    Police must have a warrant to draw the blood of a defendant who objects to the procedure.

20. T or F    A defendant has a right to counsel at a post-indictment lineup.

21. T or F    Under Title III, the Omnibus Crime Control and Safe Streets Act, an officer may obtain a court order authorizing electronic surveillance under the same rules that apply to other warrants.

22. T or F    If Merle consents to a law enforcement recording of his telephone conversation with Joan, the recording may be used at Joan's trial over her privacy invasion objection.

23. T or F    A defendant is entitled to have counsel present during a photo identification session.

24. T or F    A defendant has a Fifth Amendment right to refuse to give fingerprints.

25. T or F    If chain-of-custody is not maintained for a piece of evidence, it may not be admitted at trial.

## CHAPTER 14

1. Under federal law, arrestees are to be taken before a magistrate:

   A. Within twenty-four hours after arrest

   B. Within forty-eight hours after arrest

   C. Without unnecessary delay

   D. Immediately after the booking process has been completed

2. The purpose of a preliminary hearing is to:

   A. Be sure that the correct person has been arrested

   B. Take a defendant's plea

   C. Determine whether probable cause exists

   D. Set bail

3. A formal accusation of criminal activity by a grand jury is a(n):

   A. Indictment

   B. Information

   C. Complaint

   D. Bill of attainder

4. A formal accusation of criminal activity by a prosecutor is a(n):

   A. Indictment

   B. Information

   C. Complaint

   D. Bill of attainder

5. Generally, the purpose of the grand jury is to:

   A. Issue indictments whenever a prosecutor believes that probable cause exists

   B. Guard against unfair and arbitrary government prosecutions

   C. Acquire information, through the use of the subpoena power, that prosecutors normally cannot obtain

   D. Protect the government from the intervention of defense attorneys in the fact-finding process

6. A plea of *nolo contendere* has the same effect as a _____, except *nolo contendere* pleas _____.

   A. Guilty plea; are entered by courts for defendants who refuse to enter a plea

   B. Not guilty plea; admit the fact as stated in the charging instrument

   C. Not guilty plea; admit no civil liability

   D. Guilty plea; are not admissible in any subsequent civil trials

7. What percent of criminal cases are disposed of in the United States with pleas of guilty?

   A. 60% or less

   B. 70%–79%

   C. 80%–89%

   D. 90% or more

8. If an indictment is sufficient, but does not provide a defendant with the information necessary to adequately prepare a defense, the proper remedy is a(n):

   A. Bill of particulars

   B. Motion for clarification

   C. Motion to dismiss indictment

   D. Motion to suppress

9. The Jencks Act, 18 U.S.C. § 3500, permits defendants to inspect and copy statements of prosecution witnesses:

   A. During the pretrial discovery process

   B. At trial, before the witness testifies

   C. At trial, after the witness has testified

   D. The act prohibits such inspections

10. Which of the following must be provided to the defendant before trial under the Brady doctrine? The defendant is charged with murdering a victim with a knife.

    A. A statement of a witness claiming she saw the defendant kill the victim

B. A knife found at the scene of the crime that has the defendant's fingerprints on the handle

C. A knife found at the scene of the crime that has the fingerprints of another person on the handle

D. A statement made by the defendant confessing guilt

E. None of the above

11. The purpose of a motion in limine is to:

A. Move the trial location

B. Exclude illegally obtained evidence from trial

C. Prevent the disclosure of information to a defendant that may endanger a person's (i.e., witness's) life

D. Prevent opposing counsel from mentioning or asking questions concerning a particular subject

12. T or F    Depositions are a routine part of the criminal discovery process.

13. T or F    All defendants are entitled to have a reasonable bail set.

14. T or F    The fact that a defendant cannot pay the amount of bail set by a court does not mean it is excessive and violative of the Eighth Amendment.

15. T or F    Discovery is more limited in criminal cases than civil.

16. T or F    Under the federal rules of criminal procedure, a defendant is entitled to a copy of any scientific tests conducted by the government.

17. T or F    Reasonable bail must be made available in all cases, with one exception: when the defendant is a danger to the community.

18. T or F    Preliminary hearings are required by the United States Constitution.

19. T or F    Prisoners have no expectation to privacy while incarcerated and, accordingly, their bodies and cells may be searched at any time without any individual suspicion.

20. T or F    An alert to contraband by a well-trained and dependable dog establishes probable cause to search.

21. T or F    Officers do not need to obtain a warrant to search a home that is the site of a crime.

22. T or F    At common law, the purpose of grand jury secrecy was to protect the reputations of innocent people.

23. T or F    Today, grand juries tend to work independently and prosecutors have little influence over their decisions.

24. T or F    Discovery is broader in federal criminal cases than in federal civil cases.

25. T or F    A prosecutor may file any information against a defendant only if the defendant has been indicted by a grand jury.

## CHAPTER 15

1. In medieval England, trial by ordeal was used to determine guilt. Who was responsible for determining guilt in a trial by ordeal?

A. God

B. The defendant's friends

C. A jury made of those people who had knowledge of the case

D. The king

2. The Sixth Amendment to the United States Constitution guarantees a trial by jury:

A. In all criminal cases

B. In all felony cases

C. In all cases where the punishment may exceed six months

D. In all cases where the punishment does in fact exceed six months

3. The standard of proof in a criminal case is:

A. Beyond a shadow of a doubt

B. Beyond a reasonable doubt

C. Beyond any doubt

D. Preponderance of the evidence

E. None of the above

4. A defendant who is disorderly and disobedient may:

A. Be handcuffed

B. Be gagged

C. Be excluded from his trial

D. All of the above

E. None of the above

5. The Sixth Amendment guarantees a right to a speedy trial. As such, trials must be conducted _____ from the time the defendant is formally charged.

   A. Within three months

   B. Within six months

   C. Within one year

   D. None of the above

6. An indigent defendant has the right to appointed counsel:

   A. In all criminal cases

   B. In all criminal cases where jail time results

   C. In all criminal cases resulting in a jail term of six months or longer

   D. None of the above

7. The Sixth Amendment guarantees counsel at all:

   A. Contacts between the government and the defendant

   B. Critical stages of the proceeding

   C. Potentially inculpatory stages of the proceeding

   D. Judicial proceedings

8. Voir dire refers to what stage of trial?

   A. Jury selection

   B. Opening arguments

   C. Direct examination of witnesses

   D. Instructions to the jury by the court

9. Whenever a judge discharges a potential juror because the juror will not be fair and impartial, the judge has excused the juror:

   A. For cause

   B. Peremptorily

   C. Sua sponte

   D. None of the above

10. In *United States v. DeLuca*, 137 F.3d 24 (1st Cir. 1998), the use of anonymous juries was held to be:

   A. Per se violative of the Sixth Amendment right to a jury trial

   B. Per se violative of the Fourteenth Amendment's Due Process Clause

   C. Per se violative of the Eighth Amendment's Cruel and Unusual Punishments Clause

   D. Permissible in extraordinary situations, provided the trial takes measures to minimize the harm to the defendant

11. T or F   Unanimous verdicts are required in all criminal cases for conviction.

12. T or F   Due process requires a unanimous verdict for conviction if a six person jury is used to try a case.

13. T or F   The Supreme Court of the United States has interpreted the Sixth Amendment's Speedy Trial Clause as requiring trial within ninety days of the filing of the formal charge.

14. T or F   *Gideon v. Wainwright*, 372 U.S. 335 (1963) is important to criminal procedure because through it the Court announced that defendants have a right to compel witnesses to testify at trial.

15. T or F   The Sixth Amendment guarantees indigent defendants counsel on appeal.

16. T or F   The Sixth Amendment requires that all felonies be tried by juries of twelve persons.

17. T or F   The presumption of innocence includes the right to not appear before the jury physically restrained.

18. T or F   Defendants have no right to self-representation; however, a court may allow self-representation.

19. T or F   Both defendants and prosecutors may move for a directed verdict.

20. T or F   Allen charges have been held unconstitutional by the United States Supreme Court.

## CHAPTER 16

1. A state criminal statute requires the imposition of the death sentence for all murder convictions. The statute:

   A. Is constitutional

   B. Is unconstitutional

2. A defendant is convicted of three crimes. She is sentenced to two five-year sentences to run concurrently and a ten-year sentence to run consecutively. How much actual time was she sentenced to, not accounting for parole or other methods of early release?

A. Twenty years

B. Fifteen years

C. Ten years

D. Five years

3. Which of the following statements is true?

A. The Constitution of the United States does not guarantee a right to appeal; however, if a state provides for appeal by right, then all defendants have a constitutional right to appeal.

B. The Constitution of the United States guarantees at least one appeal in state criminal cases.

C. The Constitution of the United States guarantees appeals in all states and to all appellate courts, whether appeal is by right or discretionary.

D. The Constitution of the United States does not guarantee appeals in state criminal cases.

4. Any right a defendant has to counsel on appeal is guaranteed by:

A. The Sixth Amendment

B. The Eighth Amendment

C. The Fourteenth Amendment

D. None of the above

5. Federal habeas corpus may not be used to relitigate:

A. Fifth Amendment self-incrimination issues

B. Fourth Amendment search and seizure issues

C. Fourteenth Amendment due process issues

D. Sixth Amendment right to counsel issues

6. T or F    Lowell is charged with possession of a firearm without a permit and robbery. He is acquitted of the firearm charge but convicted of the robbery. At sentencing, the judge may factor the possession of the weapon into the sentence for the robbery conviction.

7. T or F    Under the Eighth Amendment's Fines Clause, fines must be proportionate to the offense committed.

8. T or F    The use of victim impact evidence at sentencing has been disapproved by the Supreme Court of the United States.

9. T or F    The Eighth Amendment's prohibition of cruel and unusual punishments prohibits those punishments thought by the Framers to be cruel as well as those punishments believed to be cruel today.

10. T or F    The Eighth Amendment's Cruel and Unusual Punishments Clause has been interpreted by the Supreme Court of the United States as limiting capital punishment to murderers and rapists.

11. T or F    A defendant has a Sixth Amendment right to counsel at sentencing.

12. T or F    A person need not be in physical custody to apply for federal habeas corpus relief; he only need have some restraint of liberty.

13. T or F    A state prisoner must exhaust state law remedies before applying for federal habeas corpus, even if futile.

14. T or F    Prosecutors have a limited right of appeal, while defendants enjoy a much greater right to appeal.

15. T or F    Police officers are not required to give *Miranda* warnings during routine traffic stops, even though an interrogation may occur.

# TEST BANK ANSWERS

## CHAPTER 1

1. C
2. B
3. D
4. B
5. A
6. A
7. A
8. C
9. F
10. T
11. T
12. F
13. T
14. F
15. T

## CHAPTER 2

1. C
2. B
3. A
4. B
5. B
6. B
7. B
8. A
9. D
10. D
11. F
12. T
13. F
14. F
15. F
16. T
17. F
18. F
19. F
20. T

## CHAPTER 3

1. A
2. B
3. B
4. B
5. D
6. M
7. S
8. S
9. M
10. S
11. A
12. A
13. B
14. C
15. D
16. T
17. F
18. F
19. T
20. F
21. T
22. T
23. F
24. F
25. T
26. F
27. T
28. F
29. F
30. F

## CHAPTER 4

1. A
2. B
3. C
4. D
5. D

6. C
7. B
8. C
9. C
10. C
11. B
12. C
13. F
14. T
15. F
16. T
17. F
18. F
19. F
20. T
21. F
22. F
23. F
24. T
25. T

## CHAPTER 5

1. A
2. C
3. B
4. B
5. A
6. D
7. D
8. A
9. C
10. B
11. B
12. F
13. T
14. F
15. T
16. F

17. T
18. F
19. T
20. T
21. T
22. F
23. F
24. T
25. T

## CHAPTER 6

1. B
2. B
3. B
4. C
5. D
6. D
7. A
8. A
9. A
10. B
11. F
12. F
13. T
14. T
15. T
16. F
17. F
18. F
19. T
20. F

## CHAPTER 7

1. C
2. B
3. C
4. A
5. D

6. B
7. A
8. D
9. A
10. B
11. F
12. F
13. F
14. F
15. T
16. T
17. F
18. F
19. F
20. F

## CHAPTER 8

1. B
2. A
3. B
4. D
5. C
6. B
7. B
8. D
9. A
10. B
11. T
12. F
13. T
14. F
15. T
16. T
17. T
18. F
19. F
20. T

## CHAPTER 9

1. A
2. A
3. B

4. C
5. E
6. A
7. C
8. A
9. F
10. T
11. T
12. F
13. F
14. T
15. T
16. F
17. F
18. T
19. F
20. T

## CHAPTER 10

1. F
2. T
3. F
4. F
5. T
6. T
7. T
8. T
9. B
10. C
11. A
12. C
13. B
14. C
15. A

## CHAPTER 11

1. B
2. D
3. C
4. A
5. A
6. A

7. A
8. C
9. F
10. F
11. F
12. F
13. T
14. F
15. F

## CHAPTER 12

1. B
2. A
3. B
4. D
5. C
6. A
7. B
8. D
9. D
10. A
11. T
12. T
13. T
14. T
15. F
16. F
17. F
18. T
19. T
20. F
21. F
22. T
23. F
24. F
25. F

## CHAPTER 13

1. A
2. B
3. C
4. B

5. D
6. B
7. E
8. B
9. D
10. C
11. T
12. F
13. F
14. F
15. T
16. T
17. F
18. F
19. T
20. T
21. F
22. T
23. F
24. F
25. T

## CHAPTER 14

1. C
2. C
3. A
4. B
5. B
6. D
7. D
8. A
9. C
10. C
11. D
12. F
13. F
14. T
15. T
16. T
17. F
18. F
19. F

20. T
21. F
22. T
23. F
24. F
25. F

## CHAPTER 15

1. A
2. C
3. B
4. D

5. D
6. B
7. B
8. A
9. A
10. D
11. F
12. T
13. F
14. F
15. F
16. F

17. T
18. F
19. F
20. F

## CHAPTER 16

1. B
2. B
3. A
4. C
5. B
6. T

7. T
8. F
9. T
10. F
11. T
12. T
13. F
14. T
15. T